PASS THE REINS

BRAD MCCLAIN

PASS THE REINS

AUTHENTIC COWBOY STORIES AND POEMS WITH DEVOTIONALS

Stacey McClain- Editor

Brad McClain Ministries

We remember and honor the image of the American cowboy and the freedom of his lifestyle. But the Good Book tells us that, in an ultimate sense, real freedom may only be experienced through Jesus Christ.

Jesus said that both the truth and the Son would set us free, and He was right. There is no authentic freedom without the application of absolute truth, and Jesus is both the truth and the only begotten Son of the Father, sent to save us. This is the biblical solution for our slavery to sin. We often hear, "Long Live Cowboys." The cowboy way is awesome! But nothing is better than giving praise to the One who sets us free indeed. ~ Brad

COWBOYS FREE

Across the miles and years he rides,
To chase the bovine, see,
So surprised if he could know,
What his legend came to be.

That we would so admire that life,
They lived on ranges then,
The horseback boys who drove the steers,
Across the trails back when.

A simple time with danger fraught,
For us adventure wild,
With sickness, hunger, thirst and pain,
But heroes to a child.

With full-brimmed hat and flowing scarf,
And spurs hooked to his boots,
The latigo and holstered gun,
Give dreamers cowboy roots.

Who he was and how he lived,
The art and poems show,
But deeper still the ones out there,
Who do that work and know,

That even on our best of days,
Real courage may grow thin,
He was no perfect soul at all,
But we are still his kin.

And when the horse is trotted out,
And cattle made to move,
From rising sun to when it sets,
And all is handled smooth,

We catch it and we gather in,
A page of history,
And know that somehow still we are,
The sons of cowboys free.

~~~~~~~~~~~~~~~~~~~~~~~~~~~

"So if the Son sets you free, you will be free indeed..."
John 8:36 (NIV)

~~~~~~~~~~~~~~~~~~~~~~~~~~~

"As for me and my horse, we will serve the Lord."

Brad McClain

WHAT THE COWBOYS SAY

"There's a right of passage for every cowboy. That right of passage is the opportunity to sit across the fire from those that have "been there and done that." Some of life's greatest lessons are learned in this way. Now, with this book, that blessing has been extended from a select few to anyone that has ears to hear. And at the heart of it all, this is the Gospel message. That anyone willing, not a select few, can hear and respond to the Good News. Brad McClain presents the Gospel as well as I've ever seen. Prepare your heart and dive in."

- Kevin Weatherby, Founder of Save the Cowboy

"For more than a century, cowboys have had an insatiable need to surround themselves with authenticity. I have rode with Brad and I've prayed with Brad. Here's what I've gathered about the man: Whether he's holding a rope, a pen, or the Bible, Brad is sure enough a 'hand' - a compliment earned, not given. You don't find many who're capable of speaking their seminary-training into cowboy vernacular, so I hope you'll accept the invitation to search the reckonings and ponderings found in this book to see how the Lord speaks to you. There's green pastures ahead, I promise, so get to it."

- Rusty Phillips, Cowboy/Poet

"Again, I am honored to be able to say a few words about Brad McClain's newest book, "Pass the Reins". Cowboy to the bone and God filled and inspired. Thank you, brother, for sharing this with the world!"
  - Tater Paschal, Bosque County Cowboy Church

"Brad McClain gets us! He understands those who love the Lord, love the wife, the kids and livestock in our lives. He also understands all the hardships that can go with it. I look forward to seeing the story, poem or both on the days he puts pen to paper. I'm fortunate to call him a friend."
  - Dr. Stan Cobb, Cowboy Painter

"Always a heart for God, cowboys and people on both sides of the cattle guard. Paul is reaching and teaching people the Gospel in a way we can all understand. A rare talent that he uses as a gift to others to be used by God to change lives. "
  - Dave Shumpert, X2D Ranch Ministries

"Heart. That is what I think of when I hear or read from Brad McClain. Whether he is writing or reciting a poem off the cuff, or whether he is preaching a sermon after hours and hours of research, study, and prayer, I see a man with heart. A heart for the west, and a heart that longs to please God. That's what you will find in the pages of his writing. He is a dear friend and a man of God. I know you will enjoy what you read."
  - Jeff Gore, Western Singer/Songwriter, Minister

"I think the first time I ever heard the term "wordsmith" it was referring to Chuck Swindoll, or Max Lucado, and both fill the bill. But Brad McClain is a wordsmith in his own right. The mold was cast for Brad growing up working for his dad who was a cattle order buyer. And just as being a cowboy is about heart, grit, and attitude, so is Christianity. God cast the mold and broke it when he made Brad. Brad's daily poems and devotions on "God's Horseback Gospel" are evidence of this and have touched many lives. So too, will this great book, touch many lives while letting the reader glean insight to this God gifted author."

- Bubba Fowler, Rancher/Cowboy Preacher

Brad and Bubba

PREFACE

Some of the stories you will read in this book may sound like "tall tales" or "yarns" that have been stretched over time. I can say that they are mostly true, at least from where I was sitting at the time! As Brad's younger brother, I was usually tagging along or getting pulled into some wreck just cause I was the little brother. I am so glad that there is now a record of many of our crazy experiences – my wife has often said "somebody needs to write this stuff down, you just can't make it up"! As Brad has described, we grew up in the cattle business with a father who believed in hard work and not much play. That being our world, we found the humor in almost every experience and many times turned it into a game we could enjoy. Who could rope one the fastest or outrun the other to the end of the pasture was every day fun in the midst of back breaking work. There were also plenty of lessons to be learned, if you were paying attention. Those lessons are much clearer now that we are "more mature", but still full of truth and wisdom. For the most part, neither of us ever got over the cowboy way and the enjoyment of doing a job horseback – I hope and pray we never do!

While we were trying our best to be the next world famous cow punchers, something unexpected happened – Jesus showed up and turned our world upside down. Now, we knew every Bible story that our mother had taught us since birth, but the living and powerful King of Kings got ahold of the 18 year old Brad and he was never the same. As I watched through 12 year old eyes, I saw my brother change from a cowboy to an on fire, born again, preaching machine! Brad's transformation and new direction would forever alter my life and that of my family's. Our home became a place of Bible study and prayer meetings – literally hundreds of people came to faith during those years. We still ranched and rode, but the priorities were rearranged by the power of what God was doing in our lives. We were changed forever.

All these poems that are shared in this book started from the spark of the Holy Spirit way back in those young years. I am still amazed as I read the poems and devotionals daily that Brad continues to have the inspiration of the Holy Spirit in his life. The path from young to older has not always been straight – there have been many detours, twists and turns. But one thing we know – God has been faithful through every season. Brad and I have stood shoulder to shoulder through many tough times, but we have never doubted that God was with us. I hope you will read his book and enjoy the stories that fill the chapters of our lives. More than that, I hope that Brad's poems and devotionals offer you renewed hope as you journey through your own set of stories. God bless you and good reading!

Linwood McClain

> *This book is dedicated to my family.*

For my brother, Linwood, who has always believed in me.

For my wife, Stacey, for loving me unconditionally.

For my children and grandchildren who will read these pages and catch a glimpse into my cowboy life of trials, victories and grace.

For the glory of God in Jesus name.

Brad

CONTENTS

– Road Less-Graveled
2

– "Go Back"
7

– Mimosa
11

"Cowboy Tears"
16

– Big Boy
19

– "Shame"
24

– The Hay Barn
26

– "Straight"
32

– Mama's Joy
35

CONTENTS

– "Jesus' Horses"
39

– Tap Tap Tap
42

– "Tap Tap Tap "
47

– Stockyard Cafe
51

"Stockyard Cafe"
57

– The SLE Rodeo
60

– "Hometown Rodeo"
65

– Double-hocked my Daddy
68

– "Double-hocked My Daddy"
73

– Big Cattle
77

– "Boys to Men"
80

– Dead or Alive
83

CONTENTS

— "Once Upon a Cowboy Time"
89

— Hippie
93

— "Hippie"
97

— Mendin' Fences
101

— "Work"
109

— Cotton-Eyed Joe
112

— "Stockyard Cattle"
117

— Dad's Garden
120

— "I watched"
124

— "Unplowed Ground"
128

— Covey Rise
131

— "Horse named Hallelujah"
134

CONTENTS

— Rendering Truck
138

— "Wayward Soul"
143

— Back to Texas
146

— "Zippo"
149

— Uncle Roy
152

— "Find a Way"
155

— Sell Your Saddle
159

— "He Rode "
166

— Armadillo Roping
170

— "Roping Armadillos"
175

— Pascagoula Cattle
178

— "Pascagoula Cows"
182

CONTENTS

– "Goodbye Larry Mahan'
187

– Dad's Bell
190

– "Baxter Black"
195

– Cheyenne
197

– "Amigos"
204

– Owyhee
207

– "Authentic"
213

– The Neighbor's Bull
216

– "Stumble"
222

– Last Ride
225

– "Leaving"
229

– Emu
234

CONTENTS

– "Emu "
239

– Longhorns
243

– "A Cowboy Then"
248

– Living Water
251

– "Hydrate"
256

About the Author
264
Contact Information
265

markfoleyimaging

ROAD LESS-GRAVELED

It used to be way out in the country. Before they built the by-pass, you went out Wares Ferry Road from town to get there. Dad bought the old place on Todd Road with his VA money after he came home from World War II and married my Mama. It was only three hundred twenty acres but as a kid growing up there it seemed like the Ponderosa!

When he bought it, he knew it needed a lot of work but he was ready for the job. Dad cleared the land, most of it by hand, and worked at it tirelessly. He fenced and cross-fenced it, and built a sizable barn designed to work cattle. He even built a small farm house with plans from "Progressive Farmer" magazine. It was home. Before long, the cowboy culture exploded on Todd Road. I grew up in a world of cattle, horses, tractors, trucks, cowboys, and baling hay.

Dad bought and sold cattle on commission. They were trucked to our place and sorted before the orders were completed and shipped out. Dad also leased several thousands of acres where he turned out steers for an annual grazing program. But no matter the comings and goings, Todd Road was the hub and headquarters for everything. Later, the bypass split the ranch in half. The far side we called the "New Ground" pasture. Closer in was the "Below the House" pasture and the "Hospital Pasture." These were the fields I rode as a child, checking and doctoring livestock and repairing fences.

Every Saturday morning I was in the hall of the big barn sorting cattle with Dad. On many evenings and early mornings, I was emptying pens and driving cattle up the chutes onto the trailers that the big trucks hauled to places like Emporia, Kansas and Gatesville, Texas. It was a cowboy life. It was my life.

When I was in high school, Dad lost everything in bankruptcy and we moved to a rental house in town. He became very successful in real estate and within a year was able to buy an even bigger ranch where he ran cattle for many years. Though the new place was great, Todd Road was the place I've always called home.

It has been many years since I ran those fields. The old home place has changed hands several times and now there's a Burger King in one of the pastures. Along the bypass where "New Ground" once sprung up with fresh hay, springs concrete parking lots and all sorts of businesses. It's busy and crowded with traffic. But surprisingly, the tract on the south side has not been divided or developed.

I went back to Todd Road some months ago and showed my wife where I grew up. The house burned down long ago, so it took a minute to visualize how everything used to be situated. Pecan trees that Dad planted had grown large, while others had been cut down or removed. I showed her the plot behind the house that used to be our one-acre family garden.

Up the lane to the left in the hospital pasture there still stood the large structure of a hay barn. The red paint was faded but there it was. I remember when we poured the concrete floor, over fifty years ago. As I stood among the rubble, I glanced out over the adjoining pasture. I flashed back to my teenage years to a time I was driving in horses and my horse fell down on the slick grass. That wreck gave me a concussion. I remembered having to spend the night in the hospital. Truth is, not long after I received that knot on my noggin, I became on fire for Christ and I evangelized every chance I got. I remember that my grandmother told my mama she worried that it was the blow to my head that made me act differently. I hadn't thought of that in years. I stood there a second, laughed and whispered to myself, "No, Leolin, it was Christ."

The memories flooded my mind. We walked over to what was left of the large working barn. It was falling down and there were places where trees were growing up through holes in the tin roof. I pointed out what was once the hay loft, which was the spot where I first kissed a girl.

"There used to be scales over here where we weighed the cattle." I said out loud. "And here was our saddle and tack room, the sorting alley, and large pens."

My mind flashed back to the high action that once filled this abandoned space. Snorty cattle being sorted, yearlings being run through the chute and head catch, to be branded, castrated, wormed and implanted. The faces of cowboys and day workers who came to help filled my mind.

I remembered one dusty, hot day when Dad hollered at a cow he was sorting and a fly flew in his mouth. He swallowed it while trying his best to spit it out! It gagged him good. I thought it was funny but my laughter was rewarded when a cow kicked a big clod of manure directly into my mouth the same day. Dad thought THAT was funny. Memories...

There was an old, weathered piece of wood hanging above the door that led into our old tack room with a horseshoe nailed to it. A quick pull, and it easily came loose. It became my souvenir from the old home place visit.

Though I had a piece of wood and some pics on our phone from that visit, I took away lots more than that from Todd Road. It was there that my life's foundations were laid. Yes, I went to school and church in town. But it was the fireplace, the kitchen table, the pastures, the cattle working barn, and the garden that were the places where I learned the importance of hard work, finishing what you start, keeping your word, and living right.

Places get run down and buildings deteriorate but it's what you LEARN in those places that matters most. I've traveled many miles in my life, from cities and towns, from the gulf to the plains, along freeways, skyways, pastures and dirt roads. I've lived in large homes and ranches. I've lived in trailers and even in the small corner of a barn attic. I've lived with and I've lived without. Though the miles and the adventures have been many, I will always remember home and the lessons I learned there, on the road less graveled.

~~~~~~~~~~~~~~~~~~~~~~~~~~~~~~~

> *"I don't say this out of need, for I have learned to be content in whatever circumstance I find myself. I know how to make do with little, and I know how to make do with a lot. In any and all circumstances I have learned the secret of being content- whether well fed or hungry, whether in abundance or in need. I am able to do all things through Him who strengthens me"*
> **Philippians 4:11-13 (CSB)**
~~~~~~~~~~~~~~~~~~~~~~~~~~~~~~~

"GO BACK"

Go back, go back, go way on back,
To when I was a boy,
A fifties kid, the things I did,
With a six-gun cowboy toy.

Watched cowboys close, and Roy the most,
On a black and white TV,
Three channels strong, to right the wrong,
The white hats won, you see.

A simple time, left far behind,
But when e'er I looked,
A cowboy stood, and always would,
'Twas God's plan in my book.

And then I'm grown and should have known,
What we all had back then,
Did other things but always seemed,
I'd ride and rope again.

Got older still, but like some bill,
That you can never pay,
My cowboy dreams, it always seems,
Just would not go away.

Decades gone, and was I wrong,
To love the cowboy way,
The answer's no, and time will show,
That God said it's okay.

A-horseback now and still somehow,
I find His will for me,
I've played my role, God's in control,
And He will always be.

I know it's true what we should do,
Is not our will, but His,
But what runs deep, His promise keep,
I'll also tell you this,

Identity is ours, you see,
A gift He gives us all,
And trying to, be another you,
Will only miss His call.

Whatever He calls you to be,
No matter how that plays,
Surrender all, don't fight the call,
But live it all your days.

For me to be, God's tool you see,

Means go back to my roots,

The Spirit fills and peace instills,

This man in hat and boots.

~~~~~~~~~~~~~~~~~~~~~~~~~

"You saw me before I was born. Every day of my life was recorded in your book. Every moment was laid out before a single day passed..." **(Psalm 139:16, NLT)**

God knows us, and knows what makes us tick. He gifts us with our basic DNA, personality type, and biochemistry. We do not choose our parents nor where we grow up or how, but all this is used to develop us into the person we are meant to be. Some people get the notion that Christian believers become plain-vanilla, generic clones of each other in order to gain spiritual points. The profile is bland at best. But what if all the exciting parts of who you are and what you love aren't sinful at all? What if God simply wants to harness that passion for His glory? Then would it be okay to enjoy being you? I think so, and this scripture and others like it indicate that it's all part of God's ongoing plan for us, even when we don't see it or totally understand.

Prayer Starter: Lord, lead me into who I was meant to be so that I can do what I am meant to do,

____

____

____

____

_______________in Jesus' name.
~~~~~~~~~~~~~~~~~~~~~~~~~

"Everyone who calls on the name of the Lord will be saved"
Romans 10:13 (NLT)

MIMOSA

I was three years old when my sister, Laura, was born, and it was years before we could be in the same room together without getting into a fight. I wanted a little brother and got a sister instead. My recollection is that I was often wrongly blamed and punished when it was mostly her fault. But there is one situation I remember when I was definitely wrong, though it was an accident.

When I was six years old and Laura was three Dad gave me my first full-sized horse, an old, retired steer wrestling horse named Corky. Dad said the cowboy who rode him had a cork leg and that's how Corky got his name. Was it true? Who knows? He was all black with a big, white blaze running down his face and was a perfect kid horse, gentle and very slow, although he would still watch a cow. He taught me to ride, except the getting on part was a challenge. I had to lead him alongside the fence to climb into the saddle.

Laura was always whining to ride but when she did was always complaining and fussing about something the whole time. Mama wanted me to lead her around the yard on Corky. "Yes, ma'am," I said, but I really didn't want to because little sister was such a nuisance. She put on her little red cowgirl hat and Mama helped her get up on Corky, then sent us along. I decided we would pretty much stick to the front yard which was about an acre large. Around and around we went, walking slowly beneath the outspread branches of the half-grown pecan trees Dad had planted.

All across the front of the yard nearest the road was a row of mimosa trees. They grew fast and were covered with colorful, pink, sticky blossoms. I liked 'em because they were pretty and easy to climb. So I was very familiar with these trees. It was a beautiful day. You could smell the honeysuckle on the breeze blowing from the hedge row across the road, birds flitting about, and the buzzing of honeybees as they worked the white clover blossoms in the yard.

I was walking along, slowly leading Corky when I heard Laura squalling. I turned around and she was not sitting on Corky! I looked past him to see her sitting in the grass, screaming and crying. I had led her under a mimosa branch and it had dragged her off Corky and knocked her to the ground. To make it worse, she had big plugs of grass stuck in both her nostrils. She was convinced I had done it on purpose, but I was innocent. I dropped Corky's reins and ran to the house to get Mama.

I burst in through the back door yelling, "Mama, come quick! Laura fell off!" I'm sure she feared the worst. In a panic she flew past me out the door and we both ran to where Laura had fallen. She was sitting under the mimosa tree with Corky grazing nearby and by then had settled down. She pointed at me and said, "Babo made me fall!" She called me "Babo" because I called Dad "Dado" and he called me "Brado." But she couldn't say it, so "Babo" was my nickname. Sounded like some kind of soap.

Mama was very well-acquainted with our history of conflict but first she made sure Laura wasn't hurt. Finally, after she took us both inside and poured us a Coke to drink, she looked at me and said, "Did you do this on purpose?" I said, "Mama, I promise I didn't." She believed me, and for once I didn't get sent to the peach tree for a switch.

The older we got the closer Laura and I became. As adults we got along so much better than we ever did as children. Some years ago I got a call from my brother saying that our sister and her husband were missing. They had been out on their boat that afternoon and it came ashore without them. The next day we joined a search looking for them. Later that day the body of our brother-in-law was found, and Laura's body a week later. They both drowned in what was obviously a tragic boating accident. It was a sad good-bye to say to my little sister, but I believe she's dancing the streets of heaven right now.

I've learned some things about life's accidents and tragedies, having experienced many along the way. Sometimes accidents really don't amount to much, like the low-lying mimosa limb. That only took a couple of Mama's kisses to heal. Tragedies are much more traumatic and disturbing and make us wonder why. For those it takes a lot of grace that only comes when we turn to the One who alone can heal and help us. The good news is that He is generous. He who knows us best loves us the most, and will always give us what we need. We may never forget what happens in our lives, but we CAN get THROUGH accidents and tragedies if we rely on His grace.

~~~~~~~~~~~~~~~~~~~~~~~~~~

"May the God of hope fill you with all joy and peace in believing, so that by the power of the Holy Spirit you may abound in hope." **Romans 15:13 (NIV)**
~~~~~~~~~~~~~~~~~~~~~~~~~~

"COWBOY TEARS"

Cowboys don't cry, and many such lies,
Were told to me when I was young,
My crying was rare, but just to be fair,
It was a song many have sung.

You had to be tough, and manly enough,
To hold back the things that you felt,
Just don't let it show, and let no one know,
But play the cards your life is dealt.

I guess through the years, when I didn't shed tears,
They stayed in some dark, secret place,
And then at strange times, with some desperate climbs,
They sometimes leaked right down my face.

I wiped 'em off quick, my throat would get thick,
And I'd quietly rein it away,
Hoped nobody saw, my old heart unthaw,
Wondered how to be okay.

But those sad old good-byes, and hopeless old tries,
Sometimes really touch me down deep,
Then to my surprise, tears flowed from my eyes,
I tried but I just couldn't keep,

Them all down inside, though I still tried to hide,
The emotion that loped in my soul,
But freedom, you see, is transparency,
And important if you want to be whole.

The good Book has said, and there I have read,
My tears God will bottle and keep,
If with tears we sow, there is great joy we know,
That will come with the harvest we reap.

I don't care a rip, but I'll give you a tip,
About how a cowboy should cry,
We should not keep it hid, our pride we get rid,
And to all our ego we die.

Show the boy who you are, and don't hide the scar,
Of the hurt that the Good Lord can heal,
Real men let it go, so folks can all know,
What it means to be cowboy and real.

~~~~~~~~~~~~~~~~~~~~~~~~~~~

"Those who plant in tears will harvest with shouts of joy..."
Psalm 126:5 (NLT)

The scriptures clearly place value on our tears. Psalm 56:8 tells us that God records our tears and keeps track of our sorrows. This is not to glorify emotionalism. We all know people who cry the proverbial "crocodile" tears and use emotion to manipulate others. But the genuine, sincere expression of emotion is a positive in scripture. This is especially true when we are laboring to sow righteous seed. Sometimes all you can do is get the seed in the ground, even when your heart is breaking. But joy comes with the harvest.
~~~~~~~~~~~~~~~~~~~~~~~~~~~

Prayer Starter: Lord, help us to sow with tears so as to reap a joyful harvest...

____

____
____
____
____
____
____
____
____
____
_______________________________________in Jesus' name.

BIG BOY

Every boy should have at least one good dog in his life. That's what I've always thought, anyway. I grew up watching "Lassie" and "Rin Tin Tin" on TV, so how could I feel otherwise? Mine was named "Big Boy," and he was a big, black and white English shepherd. Big Boy was not very friendly and that's what made him a good watch dog. We lived out in the country, and Dad was gone to the cattle auctions a lot, so it was good to have a canine protector on the property.

Of course growing up on a cattle ranch in rural Alabama, we had lots of dogs. Dad kept a big pack of beagles which we used to hunt rabbits every Saturday morning of the season. There were probably about ten of 'em at any given time, and though they weren't pets, all of them had colorful names. There was Drive and Mamie and Sounder, Shake, Rattle, and Roll, and Belle and Sissy to name a few. There were also cattle dogs from time to time that we used to gather livestock, and every now and then Dad would bring home some sort of pit bull cross we used to catch cattle. Life was good with lots of dogs, and Big Boy was top dog, no doubt.

Big Boy and I spent a lot of time together. He was free to roam the pastures and so was I, a perfect pair to say the least. Our days were like everything you might picture in your mind for a ranch kid's home- lots of sunshine, grassy, well-watered, rolling meadows, winding cow paths, and lots of God's creation to explore.

One time Big Boy and I ran across an old, decaying carcass of a deer on the edge of the woods. He got down in it and wallowed around and came out smelling awful! Of course I didn't care and managed to get the smell all over me, too. When we got home that day, Mama wouldn't let me in the house before she hosed me off.

I was five years old in the summer of 1958. On one of those long, hot and humid summer days I was playing outside under the big, gnarled oak tree in the back yard. No telling how old that tree was, and it was so big that three men couldn't reach around the trunk. It gave lots of shade and I enjoyed sitting under the umbrella of its branches. I rarely went barefoot because of the stickers in the yard and the cow patties in the pasture, but on this particular day I was shoeless. Flies were buzzin' and there wasn't much breeze, but in spite of the heat I decided to go for a ride on Big Boy.

I had been riding Big Boy since I was really little, and he always cooperated but I had gotten a little bigger, and this time Big Boy didn't like it. Maybe I cuffed his flank with my heel a little too hard, or maybe his tolerance was low 'cause of the weather, but he whirled around and nipped me on the heel.

He didn't bite me hard, and certainly didn't mean a thing by it, but it did break the skin a little, so I ran inside to tell Mama.

Back then every wound was treated with one thing: mercurochrome. We called it monkey blood. It was a dark red medication and I always thought of it as child abuse in a bottle, but she used it to doctor me up. She then picked up the phone to dial our pediatrician. The only phone we had was a rotary phone. It was big and black and sat by itself on a little table next to a lamp and a phone book. It was more like a small piece of furniture and I remember it actually had legs, and of course was a land line with a long cord. Our number was AM-53822. Kids now a days wouldn't understand.

Anyway, Mama stuck her finger in the holes in the round dial, turning it clockwise and slowly made the call to my doctor. Dr. Thomas Nolan took the call and explained that the only thing we had to do was pen up the dog that bit me for three days to be sure it didn't have rabies. I listened intently as Mom asked questions, and could actually hear what Dr. Nolan said. Mom hung up the phone and asked me the question I knew was coming: "Which dog bit you?"

I immediately had a moral crisis in my five year old brain. The problem was they had taken me to see the movie "Old Yeller" starring Fess Parker. You may remember the story of how the dog Old Yeller had to be killed because he contracted rabies. Somehow I thought if I told Mama that Big Boy bit me they might think he had rabies and have to shoot him. So I looked at Mama and told her a lie. It was the first lie I ever remember telling anyone.

I told Mama it was one of the beagles, Drive, that had bitten me. We went outside to find that dog and put in a pen, like Dr. Nolan had instructed. Problem was, we couldn't find that particular dog. Why? I don't know to this day, but Drive was nowhere to be found. We never did find that dog. Dad came home and we rode up and down the gravel roads and asked everyone we saw if they had seen that beagle. No one had, and Big Boy was still safe, laying in his familiar spot near the back door. I never told 'em the truth.

The next morning Mama called Dr. Nolan back and told him the news. "We can't find the dog that bit Brad," she said. "What shall we do?" "There's only one thing you can do," he said, and "it's bring Brad down here for rabies shots. There will be one a day for two weeks, fourteen in all. And we need to start right away." So that afternoon Mama put me in her 1955 Chevy sedan, and off we went downtown to Dr. Nolan's office.

The drive was long. We drove with the windows down because it had no AC and it took about forty-five minutes to get to his office. His nurse, Bessie, helped me up onto the gurney and told me to take off my shirt. Shortly, Dr. Nolan, who was one of the kindest men we ever knew, brought in the rabies shot. He had me lay down on my back, and gave me the shot under the muscle of my stomach. I cried and Mama couldn't help me. She was in the hallway with my sister.

Laura, my three year old sister, was afraid of shots so Mama had to take her to the lobby 'cause if my little sister saw a shot or had to get one, she vomited. And so it went for the next two weeks, one shot a day for fourteen days. Me on the gurney with my rabies shot and Mama in the lobby with Laura. It was a painful, time-consuming, expensive experience and one that I never forgot, though it's been sixty-plus years ago.

I didn't tell anyone the truth about Big Boy until many years later, while attending college. I guess I came to a point in my life that the little lie weighed on my conscience every time I thought about it. The good thing is that I've never had to worry about contracting rabies.

Everyone in the story is now dead but me. Mom and Dad, Dr. Nolan, Bessie, and of course Big Boy. I learned a valuable lesson at a young age, the truth can be painful but a lie hurts more.

~~~~~~~~~~~~~~~~~~~~~~~~~~~~

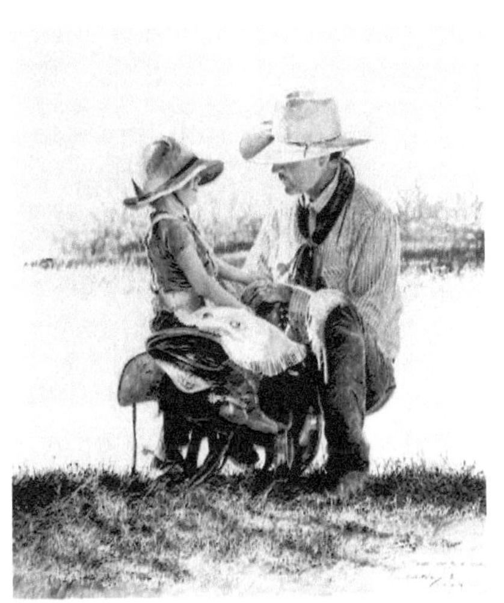
~~~~~~~~~~~~~~~~~~~~~~~~~~~~

"SHAME"

Sometimes you'd hear 'em say it,
You ought to be ashamed,
Wild horses rode, big trucks to load,
But shame, for sure, I claimed.

For years I tried to cowboy up,
And live the skills I learned,
But big regret, I bear it yet,
From time and bridges burned.

I know the Lord forgives me,
He promises He will,
I fight the shame, always the same,
I struggle with it still.

There is no condemnation,
That's how the Good Book reads,
But that old noise, accusing voice,
Still plants those guilty seeds.

I hear God speaking comfort,
To say it's all His grace,
We can rest, His love the best,
To help us run the race.

The voice of God's own Spirit,
Inside to give us peace,
That burden gone, we bore so long,
And from all shame release.

~~~~~~~~~~~~~~~~~~~~~~~~~~~

"Therefore, there is now no condemnation for those who are in Christ Jesus, because through Christ Jesus the law of the Spirit who gives life has set you free from the law of sin and death." **Romans 8:1-2 (NIV)**

What is the law of sin and death? It is simply that we have sinned against God and are guilty of breaking God's law. The penalty for our sin is death, which is broadly defined as separation from God. To be condemned means to be judged guilty. The Good News of Jesus Christ is that we have been pardoned and now judged "not guilty" because of what Jesus did for us. Through His death and resurrection we are totally forgiven and made right with God, and therefore are set free from all condemnation. The Spirit of life makes it so, and speaks to us with certainty that we are forgiven. Sometimes it takes awhile for this to set in, however. Shame can be used by the enemy to keep us bogged down. No condemnation means no condemnation.

Prayer Starter: Lord, help me to realize that I no longer have the bear the burden of shame, in Jesus' name.
~~~~~~~~~~~~~~~~~~~~~~~~~~~

THE HAY BARN

There was a big old red barn my Dad and Grandaddy built on our place on Todd Road. Everything in it was designed to work cattle. It had a center alley with large pens on each side. The loading docks for both upper and lower trailer decks were to the right. There was a saddle room, small office, and weighing scales to the left. The barn had a long working chute with a squeeze and head catch at the end. There was a huge hay loft overhead with openings over the hay racks below to feed the cattle. They added onto it and expanded several times through the years before they finally decided that another barn was needed to store hay.

There were small pastures or "traps" surrounding the large barn where cattle were kept short-term to be doctored or held till they were shipped out. The "hospital pasture" was one of them, and that's where Dad decided they would build the new hay barn.

It was magnificent. It was rectangular in shape, about fifty feet wide and about two hundred fifty feet long. It was at least fifty feet tall, with sheet metal siding painted red, and a concrete floor. The space was cavernous inside, not divided or partitioned in any way, just a big, open area to store hay, or if needed, to park equipment. It had big, sliding doors on both ends but no other windows or openings. I was just a kid when they built it, but I thought it was the biggest, nicest barn I'd ever seen. I especially loved the concrete floor!

The hospital pasture always had a few cattle in it that had to be doctored on a daily basis. We also had to do a daily head count, which was one of Dad's requirements. "How did they look?" he'd ask. "Did you get a head count?" God help you if you forgot to count 'em.

One Saturday morning I got up early and smelled bacon frying. I pulled on my boots and went to the breakfast table. Dad had smoked up the kitchen and was cracking eggs into the grease. We even had cheese toast, which he asked me to pull out of the oven. Mom and my younger brother and sister were still asleep so me and dad had a feast without them and then we headed out to start the day.

The pastures were dark and foggy. Dad said, "Brad, the first thing I want you to do is check the hospital pasture. Take a syringe with you (I always did) and give shots to those that need it. Sid will help you if you need him. And make sure you get a head count."

As always, I answered with a loud, "Yessir!"

I went up to the barn office and got medicine and a syringe, then walked the hospital pasture. The hospital pasture wasn't very big and since it was close to the barn, I did everything on foot. Most of the time you could corner an animal and give it a shot in the hip before it could get away from you. That day I even gave shots to a couple of yearlings that didn't want to get up.

When I was done with the doctorin', I counted all of them. There were fourteen head. Fourteen. I immediately knew something was wrong because there was supposed to be fifteen. I counted them again. Yep. Fourteen. One was missing.

I walked the entire lot looking for the missing bovine. I checked the fences for any place he could have escaped. I made sure all the gates were fastened shut. The missing calf was a Hereford crossbred and was the wildest in the bunch. He had vanished. I hated to tell Dad, for obvious reasons, and he was irritated when I told him that I couldn't find the calf.

"Go back out there and look again," he said. You didn't argue with Dad when he gave an order so I headed back to the search.

I went and walked the lot again but came up empty. I really hated to tell Dad that I couldn't find him. When he saw me coming, he asked, "Where did you find him?"

"I couldn't find him," I quietly responded.

"Did you walk the fences and check the gates?"

"Yessir, I did."

He paused for a while and then said, "Come with me." We then walked the hospital pasture together. No Hereford cross calf in sight. "I'll be derned," Dad said. "Where is that fool?" "Go, saddle your horse, Brad. I want you to ride every lot and pasture on this place till you find him."

Again, I responded with a, "Yessir!" There was always a "yessir".

It was a fine, sunny September day. I caught my dun horse, Dizzy, saddled him and started riding the adjoining lots. I then rode the larger pastures and covered two of them before dinner. By "dinner", I mean lunch. We called lunch "dinner" back then and we called the evening meal "supper".

When we sat down to eat dinner, Dad asked if I had found the yearling. I had to tell him no and proceeded to tell him the pastures where I had looked. Dad shook his head and muttered something under his breath. I covered the rest of the place that afternoon. Still no yearling...

A couple days went by and the mystery of the missing calf went unsolved. On Tuesday afternoon after I got home from school, Sid, our foreman, asked if I could help him move some hay. Not exactly my favorite thing, but I obliged and was quick to help.

When we pulled the hay truck out to the new barn, I jumped out and started to open the sliding door. I noticed it wasn't closed completely. There was a two-foot gap at the far end and when we opened it, we heard some commotion from inside.

The sound was coming from high up in the stacked hay. When I say high up I mean almost to the ceiling. As our eyes followed the sound up the mountain of coastal, we spotted him. It was the missing yearling, with only his head peering over the cliff of hay!

How he climbed up so high in the stacked hay, no one could say, but he was stuck up there and couldn't get back down. We stood there and scratched our heads a bit. I asked, "How are we going to get him down, Sid?"

"Grab your rope," Sid answered.

I retrieved my rope, and we climbed up in the hay and got a lariat loop around his head, then made a halter so we could pull him out without choking him. We pulled and pulled but he didn't budge.

Finally, we moved enough hay around to make a little path for him, then tied the end of the rope to the trailer hitch ball on the truck, and eased the truck forward, slowly. It worked like magic and the yearling came down out of the hay. We led him to the watering trough and let him go.

I had to wait for hours to tell Dad that we had found that crazy calf. Dad always worked the sale in Selma, Alabama every Tuesday, and they had big fall runs that day, so Dad didn't get home till almost 10:00 PM. That night, Mama let me stay up to tell Dad the story about our great adventure in the hay barn. He just shook his head and laughed about it. Every cattleman knows that lost and found is a big, recurring theme on a cattle ranch. It's that way in life, too.

As I ventured down the hall to bed that night, I swore I heard Dad whistling as he sorted through his cattle bills. Amazing Grace comes to mind. "I once was lost, but now am found; was blind, but now I see".

~~~~~~~~~~~~~~~~~~~~~~~~~~~

~~~~~~~~~~~~~~~~~~~~~~~~~~~

"STRAIGHT"

I try to plow my furrows straight,
And pull a line for posts,
I don't want hurry to negate,
What I desire the most.

To do things right, deliberate,
And correctly get it done,
But oftentimes I clearly state,
I'll get off track, old son.

A little off but not by much,
At first you cannot tell,
But go a ways the crooked touch,
Will point you straight to hell.

But I have a promise,
I think I have this right,
And I am being honest,
And looking to the light.

Trust in the Lord with all my heart,
That's how the Good Book reads,
Acknowledge Him, He'll do His part,
And help me with my needs.

He'll give me wisdom and will guide,
To take the path that's straight,
And when I waiver I'll confide,
His grace for me is great.

There's a straight and narrow way,
That few can seem to find,
But it is there and what I say,
Is don't be left behind.

"Trust in the Lord with all your heart and lean not on your own understanding; in all your ways acknowledge Him, and He will make your paths straight." **(Proverbs 3:5-6, NIV)**

Straight paths are what we need. God's recipe for receiving this from God involves three things: trust in the Lord, don't lean on your own understanding, and acknowledge Him in everything. These combine to position us to receive God's guidance, the straightening of our paths. Only God can untie our knots and replace confusion with direction. But it only comes when we trust Him wholeheartedly, refuse to counsel ourselves, and surrender control to Him. This is not always easy but it's always worth it.

Prayer Starter: Lord, help me. Straighten my path, Lord. In Jesus' name. Amen!

Mama and Dad

MAMA'S JOY

Mama loved everybody. She really did, and people loved her in return. She was a joyous, compassionate, non-judgmental woman, except when it came to drinking liquor. She was against it and would let you know how she felt. For many years her main message was get saved and get sober. She often said, "I just don't approve of drinking." When I was a little boy I sometimes said, "Yes, ma'am, but even Matt Dillon and Doc Adams and Festus drink beer on "Gunsmoke," and they're the good guys." "I don't approve of that," she'd say. One time I said, "Mama, Jesus turned water into wine, and his mama told him to do it." "I don't approve of that, either," she said.

The year Dad went bankrupt and lost the ranch, Mama became very depressed. We moved into a rent house in town and Dad started selling real estate. Her lifelong best friend, Helen, invited her to come stay with her in Florida for a few days. When she came back Mama talked about people being Spirit-filled, and attending a number of large prayer meetings where these people worshipped the Lord in a powerful way. About that same time, my junior year of high school, a Spirit-filled man came to our church for a weekend meeting. I had a life-changing encounter with the Lord at an overnight youth retreat, along with a handful of others.

We began having a youth Bible study led by my mother. The group went from thirty to three hundred within a few weeks. It was an amazing thing to see, and the numbers continued for an entire year. During that time Dad regained his feet financially and was able to buy another ranch. He continued selling real estate but got back in the yearling business. Young people would find their way to our new home in the country for Bible study or to just sit at Mama's table and talk.

One night at a church in town, Mom was leading a Bible study for a group of high schoolers when a very large and very smelly young man came in. No one knew him. Turns out he had been on the road for a while, was on his way to Florida, and had run out of money. He had red hair and a bushy beard and was very ominous looking. When time came for testimonies he stood up and in a very angry tone, cursed out the entire group! Everyone was pretty shocked, and then he stormed out of the room and slammed the door behind him. Mom called for a prayer, and then several more people shared their stories of God's love before the meeting ended. Afterward everyone was hanging around talking. The guy had stayed in the parking lot, and had nowhere to spend the night. Mom invited him to the country.

After a hot shower, clean clothes (too small 'cause they belonged to Dad), two bowls of my Mom's beef stew with cornbread, and a huge piece of caramel pound cake, the old boy was ready to listen. Sitting there at her kitchen table, Mama told Ted Vail about the life, death and resurrection of Jesus Christ. She explained how each of us can be saved if we are willing to turn from our sins and put our trust in the Savior. And that is exactly what happened to Ted.

His life radically changed and he stayed with us for a while until he could find work and his own place. He was from Boston and had never been around cattle or horses before. Dad put him to work anyway. He didn't know enough to be scared, and one time he stepped on a green horse that promptly bucked him off on his head. He was pile-driven head-first into a big ant bed. This made him a little more careful the next time. At our Bible studies Ted always wanted to say what had happened to him. Problem was, it took a while for him to get his language cleaned up. Mom would just laugh and say, "Now, Ted, you know you can't use those words here." And he'd always say, "Yes, ma'am. Sorry, but I got excited and forgot."

Only the Lord knows how many people found their way home to God through my Mama's kitchen. Time passed. The ranch was sold, Dad died, and Mom remarried Tommy, her childhood sweetheart. They had ten happy years together before Tommy went to join the Lord.

After Tommy died, we lost my sister in a drowning accident. Shortly afterwards, Mama showed signs of dementia. Eventually her memory became more and more limited. She had to be cared for in a special facility, and that's where she spent her final days, sleeping most of the time. I got to be with her just before she died, and always wore my cowboy hat when I went there. She knew who I was when she saw it and had joy to the end. Mama was ninety-four when she crossed over, and heaven is more real to me because she's there.

After the funeral I was praying and thinking about Mom. In all the years, I had never seen my mother ride a horse. She loved them, and loved for us to ride them, but I never saw her sit on one at all. As I prayed I caught a glimpse of my mother in heaven. She was young again, with long, flowing brunette hair to her shoulders, and she was riding a galloping horse! The sun was shining, and the trees were beautiful and the wind was blowing. She was looking over her shoulder at Jesus, who was riding along beside her. They were laughing as they rode...

~~~~~~~~~~~~~~~~~~~~~~~~~

"Then I saw heaven opened, and behold, a white horse! The one sitting on it is called Faithful and True..."
Revelation 19:11 (ESV)

~~~~~~~~~~~~~~~~~~~~~~~~~

"JESUS' HORSES"

Out yonder in tomorrow,
Where yet I cannot go,
Though now I deal with sorrow,
One thing I'm sure I know,

That there's a good horse waiting,
Made just for me to ride,
And there is no negating,
Though the devil might have tried.

But no way he will stop me,
On the ride the Lord has planned,
It is a future memory,
For me that fire is fanned.

Based upon a promise,
That was made once long ago,
And I'm no doubting Thomas,
It's by the Spirit that I know,

That the horse, he is a white one,
And I'll bet athletic, too,
With a wide hip, can't be outrun,
And a pretty head, it's true.

And right there 'longside others,
Is the one the Lord will ride,
With all the sisters and the brothers,
Praise rising like the tide.

The riders altogether,
When the Lord of hosts appears,
Evil will be tethered,
And He'll dry our every tear.

Out yonder in tomorrow,
It's my future memory,
When Jesus' horses will show,
The end of history.

~~~~~~~~~~~~~~~~~~~~~~~~
~~~~~~~~~~~~~~~~~~~~~~~~

"The armies of heaven, dressed in the finest of pure white linen,
followed Him on white horses..."
Revelation 19:14, NLT

| 41 |

The Bible speaks of a day in the future when Jesus will return to earth and end human history as we know it. He will reign, and every tongue will confess Him as Lord and every knee will bow to Him. He will ride from the heavenly realm on a great white horse, and those who have become part of the great heavenly host of believers will also ride on white horses. The magnitude and magnificence of this event is beyond all description, but it's coming. The thought of it should make our hearts beat faster with anticipation! Never doubt it. Jesus is coming again.

Prayer Starter: Lord, help me live with joyous anticipation of the day when You will return,

____

____

____

____

____

____

in Jesus' name.

TAP TAP TAP

Dad had me working cattle as soon as I was able to open and close a gate. Cattle had to be sorted in the alleyway of the barn. A group of them would be let out of a pen and driven to the end of the alley. I would be assigned a gate and when Dad cut out an animal, he shouted, "Brad, catch!" I was supposed to open my gate, which would allow the cow to go into the pen where they belonged. This was something we typically did every Saturday morning but also at other times. Often the different orders of cattle were mixed together on the cattle trailer when they were hauled in from the stockyard, hence the need to separate the various kinds according to the appropriate orders. Catch and pass was how we did it.

All of this was done on foot, though we sorted cattle in the larger lots outside the barn a-horseback. Dad used a cattle whip to cut out the cattle, one head at a time. Sometimes the cattle were hard to handle. Some were very wild and snorty, and would run over you if they could. Sometimes they were so fast it was hard to get the gate open quick enough to let them into the pen. You didn't want one to get by you, if at all possible. If one did, it was never a good thing. Dad became very agitated while working cattle. It was important that you were alert and respond quickly to his shouts.

At a young age, six or seven years old, I showed a skill for sorting cattle. Maybe it was just from watching Dad, but I had a knack for anticipating what they were going to do before they did it. Dad noticed, but never praised me for it. My proficiency was something he expected. Maybe it was for this reason that, as I got older- twelve, thirteen, fourteen- I was given the responsibility of loading the trucks.

When a buyer purchased cattle, I was responsible to help load the trucks for the drivers who came to haul cattle away. If they got there during the day, there was a whole crew of people who could do it. Oftentimes, however, the drivers arrived in the middle of the night.

Delays were common with cattle trucks and of course, there were the accidents. One truck, hauling a load on an icy winter night, had a wreck coming through Birmingham, Alabama. The driver jumped clear as the truck and trailer rolled over seven times down Red Mountain. Many of the cattle were killed or injured, but probably half the load escaped into the upscale neighborhoods nearby. Cattle had to be roped out of back yards, swimming pools, and broad city boulevards before it was over. That was a huge mess.

One time one of our drivers ran his load under a low overpass in Georgia late one night. When the state trooper called Dad, he immediately enquired about the safety of our driver. "Was John, my driver, hurt?" he asked. The state trooper responded, "We think he's okay, but he won't get out of the truck." "Why not?" Dad asked. The trooper laughed and told Dad, "He just sits there in the cab and says, 'Lord, have mercy,' over and over." Everything turned out ok but it is a wonder it didn't happen more than it did.

Our best driver was a giant of a man named George McCall. George worked for my Dad for many years, and built a quiet reputation for getting the job done. Soft-spoken and with a big ready smile, George always asked me how I was doing and if my Mama was doing okay. He had old-school southern manners. Lord only knows how physically strong he was. He had several prominent scars on his forearms and one on his neck. He explained that he was pretty wild as a young man and had survived several knife fights. I had no reason to doubt him.

All the drivers knew where my bedroom was located in the house. Dad would leave me the paperwork on the cattle before he went to bed with a note saying what pen held them and how many there were. "Do you have any questions, son?" he'd say. "No sir," I always replied. I learned pretty quickly it was better NOT to ask questions. Invariably if you did, Dad would get impatient and say he was going on to bed.

The fact that he trusted me to handle this kind of chore made me feel proud. Thousands of dollars worth of livestock were being shipped out for Texas or Kansas or Oklahoma or wherever, and I was the one getting the job done.

Many times, way over in the middle of the night there would be a tap, tap, tap on my bedroom window. The drivers always used their flashlight to wake me up. The first time it happened, I woke up in a panic to see a six foot, five inch giant staring through my bedroom window. It was George McCall and he was smiling at me. I calmed down, pulled on my jeans and cowboy boots, and met George on the back porch.

That big old Freightliner was running and all the trailer lights glowed brightly in the summer night. He backed up to the loading chutes and I flipped on the barn lights and found the cattle. It was a bunch of crossbred yearlings headed for Gatesville, Texas. George met me in the hall of the barn with a hot shot in his hand. "How many you want on the first cut?"

I walked back to the pen, opened the gate, and cut out fifteen head. I drove them up the loading chute and into the trailer. George threw the gate, and so it went. There were two more cuts on the bottom deck and two for the top. When the cattle were loaded I gave George the paperwork. He smiled and said, "Thank you, Brad. You did good tonight. I didn't have to wait on no cattle at all."

"Thanks, George," I said. "You drive safe."

He chuckled a southern, "I sho will." And off he went.

I closed the driveway gate behind him, and stood and listened to him shift gears in the Freightliner until all I could hear was the crickets again. A cool breeze blew across my face. This was the time of night when the summer heat cooled down enough to breathe in Alabama.

I slipped back into the house, leaving my boots outside on the steps. I washed up, then crept back into my bed. In what seemed like a minute or two, I heard the voice of my Dad calling us to the breakfast table. "Breakfuh!" he shouted. It was six AM, and I had been back in bed since 2:45 A.M. Though I barely had three hours of sleep, the smell of bacon made me happy and I looked forward to the next time a driver tapped on my window. That time feels like a long time ago.

Looking back on it now, I sometimes think about everything that was entrusted to me as a kid. I was raised to work. I was taught responsibility. I was taught respect. I wasn't entitled. I wasn't lazy. A cowboy never was. A cowboy never is. I wasn't paid an allowance for chores or loading cattle trucks in the middle of the night but what I WAS given were memories that I will always treasure.

Hard work is a gift. If you know, you know. Truth is, some of my fondest memories were working the late nights in the catch pens following the distinctive rapping at my window.... Tap, tap, tap...

~~~~~~~~~~~~~~~~~~~~~~~~~
~~~~~~~~~~~~~~~~~~~~~~~~~

"TAP TAP TAP "

At my window there was tapping,
Tap, a-tap, tap, tap,
And I jumped up and into jeans,
Pulled on cowboy boots and hat.

Grabbed my flashlight from the table,
And the note Dad left for me,
And out into the darkness,
To meet our driver, don't you see.

And he backed up that big rig,
While I turned on the lights,
Went to the pen of cattle,
That were going to leave that night.

And cut by cut I brought 'em,
Up the chute and on the truck,
And soon the truck was loaded,
And if we were in luck,

The driver hauled those cattle,
Where they were s'posed to go,
I'd clean up, go back to bed,
And soon wake up you know.

And Dad would ask how did it go,
While he spooned eggs on my plate,
And if the driver was on time,
Or if he had run late.

And then he'd go to auctions far,
To buy another load,
And I'd be off to school or what,
The next chore for me showed.

Sometimes I hear the tap, tap, tap,
It wakes me from my sleep,
But there's no one at my window,
And I think about it deep.

The Bible says the Lord will knock,
And wants to come on in,
For those who don't yet know Him,
Or those who've lukewarm been.

And if we open up the door,
He fellowships and stays,
Never late, our load to bear,
And makes our lives okay.

A little childhood lesson,
From years and years ago,
When I heard the driver tapping,
And now I surely know,

That the Lord will let us hear Him,
When He taps and calls our name,
And if we let the Savior in,
We'll never be the same.

~~~~~~~~~~~~~~~~~~~~~~~~~~~

"Look! I stand at the door and knock..."
Revelation 3:20 (NLT)

John's revelation describes Jesus knocking at the door, with the promise that if the door is opened He will come in and share a meal as friends. It's a powerful picture of the God who desires intimacy with us, and proactively seeks to have a personal relationship with us. It is in the closeness of that relationship that all sins are forgiven, all addictions broken, and all hurts healed. He wants to come in so that He is given permission to do all these things for us. But He will not force His way in. The door must be intentionally and decisively opened by us. In other words, all He is really asking for is cooperation. How about it? Are you willing to cooperate with the One who can solve everything for you and change your life?

Prayer Starter: Lord, help me open the door and let You in,

____

____

____

______________ in Jesus' name.
~~~~~~~~~~~~~~~~~~~~~~~~~~~

"Sing to God, you kingdoms of the earth, sing praise to the Lord, to him who rides across the highest heavens, the ancient heavens, who thunders with mighty voice." **(Psalm 32-33 NIV)**

STOCKYARD CAFE

The Capitol Stockyard Café in Montgomery, Alabama was not a very big place as I recall. When you entered the front lobby of the sale barn to the left was the office with big wooden counters where the buyers and sellers and drivers checked in. To the right, just past the shoe shine stand, was a door over which hung a hand-painted white sign with red letters that read "Café." Going through that door was always special for me.

I went there with my Dad. He worked out of town sales early in the week- Robertsdale on Monday, Selma on Tuesday, and Birmingham on Wednesday. On Thursday it was different places and later, a local sale called Hooper Stockyard on the west side of town. Every Friday, for years and years, he worked the old Capitol Stockyard sale on Furnace Street in north Montgomery.

The old-style stockyard café had character. The floor was black and white linoleum and in the front windows, facing the gravel parking lot, hung dust-covered venetian blinds. There was a short counter with stools on one side and maybe a dozen tables spread across the room. The tables were sturdy steel and chrome affairs. A thick piece of glass covered the top of each one.

The short glass counter near the door was covered with faded business cards of cattle ranches, order buying companies, feed and equipment sales, mechanic shops, and a random assortment of others. An ancient cash register sat atop that old counter. Next to it, a jar of peppermint candy with a little sign that said "take one". Then of course there was the tooth pick dispenser that gave you one at a time when you pressed down. Not everybody took a peppermint, but most got a tooth pick. I would always grab a couple extra to stick in my hat band for later use.

When you walked in, you immediately went from the faint smell of cattle manure of the sale barn to the strong smell of coffee and cigarette smoke. There was an ash tray on every table, but since the ceilings were twelve feet high, the blue haze hung there and made it tolerable for non-smokers.

The walls of the stockyard café held hundreds of stories. There was an old rodeo poster of the first SLE in 1958. The "Gray Ghost" from the old television series was the featured star. I was only six years old, but I was there for the beginning of our hometown rodeo. There was a big, old Charlie Russell print of cowboys trying to tame a bronc.

There were dozens and dozens of photographs, many of them framed. Serious men with cowboy hats stood beside a young person holding the lead rope of a fat Hereford show calf, no doubt the county winner that year. Young, skinny rodeo cowboys, cigarettes dangling, stood smiling in front of bucking chutes and one holding a buckle he won in the bull riding. At the bottom someone had penned the words Bonifay, Florida.

There was a picture from the Turtles Rodeo Association, someone riding a bronc at Madison Square Gardens, I think it was. There were pictures of cutting horses, roping horses, race horses, and draft horses. There were poster advertisements for Tony Lama boots that Jimmy Alverson would sell you across the street at the Montgomery Serum Company, cowboy headquarters in our part of the world. There were posters selling feed, fertilizer, equipment, and Martha White's self-rising flour.

My Dad seemed to know a lot of the people In the pics. He would point someone out in one of the photos and say, "See that fella there?"

"Which one, Dad?", I would ask.

He'd always say, "Look where I'm pointing, Brad."

I knew to answer, with my quick, "Yessir."

"I knew that cowboy's daddy. He's from here but married a Texas gal. They ran lots of cattle both here in Alabama and near Gatesville, Texas. I sold him several loads of cattle." Then Dad would get a faraway look in his eye and say, "He died a couple of years ago and I believe his widow sold their place here and moved back to Texas." Any conversations like that always happened before the food came. Dad ate quickly and didn't linger long at the table afterward.

The food at the Capitol Stockyard Café was memorable and was mostly fried. The fried chicken, fried green tomatoes, and fried okra were the best. 'Course they served a really good cheeseburger, a pulled pork barbeque sandwich, and a BLT piled so high with bacon that you would almost founder if you ate it all. They had a blue plate special for lunch which included your meat – fried catfish or meatloaf or calf liver or whatever, your three sides, sweet tea, and a dessert. They even served a pretty decent ribeye that would be considered prime by today's standards but then was only good to choice.

As far as I remember, it was the only place in Montgomery where you could get calf fries. Once we were eating in a swanky place in Atlanta visiting my uncle when my little brother Linwood asked for mountain oysters. They didn't have 'em, but the waiter found it humorous. The ones at the stockyard were really good.

The desserts were to die for, my favorite being chocolate pie with a big layer of meringue on top. But honestly, their best food was for breakfast. It was epic southern fare- eggs however you liked 'em, patty sausage, bacon piled high, grits (no hashbrowns), cat-head biscuits, gravy, and sliced tomatoes.

I never saw but two people working at the stockyard café. There was the short order cook and one waitress. Looking back I wonder how they handled everything, but they did. One kept the food coming and the waitress did everything else. Maybe it's because they were only open Thursday through Saturday and only served breakfast and lunch, but they made it happen.

I cannot remember the waitress's name. I think it was something different like Wyelda or Estelle or maybe Freddis. I do remember she had dyed red hair with a net over it, blue eye shadow, red lipstick to match her hair, and a gold tooth right in the front. She was a large woman, and wore a white uniform. She called everyone "darlin" or "sweetheart" and kept everyone's coffee cup or sweet tea filled, while serving food and bussing the plates after. She always was cheerful and smiling with an easy laugh, but was the kind you wouldn't want to cross.

The cook was a giant of a man who learned to cook in the Navy, had done prison time and hauled cattle when he was not cooking. Everyone highly regarded him. People were willing to take a number and wait in the stockyard lobby if there wasn't a seat. It was that kind of place.

The day of the stockyard café is almost past in most places. The old Capitol Stockyard closed many years ago. I hear the café stayed open for awhile after but didn't make it. The stockyard across town is now closed, too, and it's really hard to believe there is no cattle auction in Montgomery, Alabama when thousands of livestock were sold there through the years.

Fast food restaurants and Cracker Barrel chain stores have replaced the old cafes of my childhood. Though those days are far and the places are few, I still go there in my memory, where men sat together, told stories, drank coffee and made thousand dollar cattle deals with only their word and a handshake.

Isaiah 55:11 (NKJV), tells us, "*So shall My word be that goes forth from my mouth; It shall not return to Me void. But it shall accomplish what I please; And it shall prosper in the thing for which I sent it*"

In other words, God doesn't make empty promises. If He has given you a word on something, you can trust Him. We too should stand on these principals. His Word is His bond. So too should ours.

~~~~~~~~~~~~~~~~~~~~~~~~~

Brad and Leo (grandson)
~~~~~~~~~~~~~~~~~~~~~~~~~

"STOCKYARD CAFE"

It's a place I can remember,
I'd like to go back to,
It's that old stockyard cafe,
I recall when it was new.

My Dad, a cattle buyer,
Made an auction every day,
But the sale barn in our home town,
Had this little old cafe.

A set of horns up on the wall,
And a Charlie Russell print,
One side filled with photographs,
Of cowboys 'fore they went.

Sometimes Dad would name 'em,
And say somethin' that he knew,
'Bout this old hand or that one,
The memories fairly flew.

The buyers and the big shots,
Mixed in with all the rest,
Cowboys, day hands, drivers,
I liked auctioneers the best.

Many deals were done there,
And cattle bought and sold,
Many lies and stories,
Were laughed at back when told.

I was just a youngster,
But wide-eyed took it in,
Broncs and outlaw cattle,
And those weather-beaten men.

The coffee there was strong and black,
And so was Jane the cook,
Man, she could fill your table,
With down-home tastes and look.

The gravy there was awesome,
The steak was country-fried,
Vegetables and corn bread,
And God's best apple pie.

No one got too worried,
When a cigarette was lit,
Roll your own Bull Durham,
Or a chew someone would spit.

I guess it was a different time,
And now we've moved on past,
Heard they tore the stockyard down,
Things change, and some don't last.

But I'll always remember,
That place where we would eat,
Where a way of life was honored,
And cowboys came to meet.

~~~~~~~~~~~~~~~~~~~~~~~~~~~~
~~~~~~~~~~~~~~~~~~~~~~~~~~~~

"...People are like grass; their beauty is like a flower in the field. The grass withers and the flower fades. But the word of the Lord remains forever..." 1 Peter 1:24 (NLT)

THE SLE RODEO

The Southeastern Livestock Exposition (SLE) Rodeo started in 1958 when I was 6 years old. For as long as I can remember, the annual rodeo has always been a big deal to me. Maybe it was because my Dad's ranch was just a few miles from Garrett Coliseum, in Montgomery, Alabama, my home town. Maybe I looked forward to the rodeo, not only for the cowboy competitions, but also because it was one of the few things my dad allowed himself to enjoy every year. He was working hard as a cattle buyer for every other part of the year. Dad didn't go to my childhood sporting events or my 4-H shows, but he took me to the rodeo when I was very young, and I never got over it.

One of the things I remember about the early years of the rodeo was the western television stars who always came to perform. These were the very ones we watched on Saturday mornings and weekday evenings and it was amazing to me. One of the first that I remember was Gail Davis, star of the popular "Annie Oakley" series.

We had lots of "Gunsmoke" stars including, Dennis Weaver (Chester), Milburn Stone (Doc Adams), Amanda Blake (Miss Kitty), and my favorite, Ken Curtis (Festus). Festus always surprised us with his beautiful baritone singing voice.

We had Lorne Green who played Ben Cartwright on "Bonanza," Dale Robertson from "Wells Fargo", Fess Parker who played both Davy Crockett and Daniel Boone, Rex Allen, the singing cowboy, and Clint Eastwood, who played Rowdy Yates on "Rawhide." As kids, we ran down the steps to the fence encircling the arena to shake hands with the stars when they rode by. They were larger than life!

Every year in March our schools closed for what they called the AEA holiday. It was for the Alabama Education Association, so teachers could have a two-day spring break. I got to be out of school all week because I showed 4-H calves and rode in the grand entry of the rodeo every night.

At the beginning of the week our ranch foreman, Sid, would haul my two steers to the show barns on the rodeo grounds. We'd have a county show first, then the state show. I showed my steers in both, then sold them at the big sale at the end of the week. Until they sold, I took care of the calves each day with feed, water, grooming and mucking stalls. I also took my buckskin horse, Dizzy, and put him in a stall for the entire week.

When I wasn't fooling with my calves, I was riding my horse around the rodeo grounds, watching the cowboys and talking to people. Each night of the rodeo, I lined up with hundreds of other riders for the grand entry. It was at the beginning of each performance, and led by Dr. Phil Hardy, who always wore a green sport coat.

I loved the Grand Entry. I never missed. It always got a little wild and western because they allowed the public to participate with whatever horse they wanted to bring. I've seen lots of horses get sideways through the years.

One year, my brother Linwood and I worked up enough nerve to enter the team roping. We figured since we had spent a lot of time roping pasture yearlings, practicing at our home arena and roping in local jack pots, we might as well give it a go.

They had the team roping on Saturday morning during the slack, and I can't remember ever feeling more nervous. I backed my good gray gelding, Drifter, into the roping box and Linwood, who was heeling, got all set. He was riding our buckskin mare, Dusty. I nodded for the steer and almost immediately the fellows around the chutes hollered, "Go, go, go!"

At the sound of the chute release, I spurred Drifter and he was so quick he literally jumped over the barrier rope like a steeple-chaser! I barely had my seat when I threw at the steer and, of course, I missed. I was so embarrassed I rode out of the arena leaving my good, silver belly Resistol hat behind. Someone had to retrieve it and bring it to me. When they handed it to me, I noticed that my horsehair hatband was missing. I assumed it was buried in the dust of the arena. I's a bittersweet memory, but I can always say I roped at the SLE.

As the years went by, the SLE rodeo declined in popularity. The old Garrett Coliseum needed maintenance and repairs. Regrettably, the grounds were also neglected. The cattle business even shifted away from Montgomery. Where there were once two big stockyards in the heart of Montgomery, today there are none. The Alabama Wagon Train disbanded. It once began near Boaz in north Alabama and riders rode 165 miles to the rodeo. Today it is a distant memory. The downtown rodeo parade was discontinued as well. Things were looking bad for my hometown rodeo.

A few years ago. things began to shift in a more positive direction. The popularity of the Cowboy Channel, RFD-TV, and TV's "Yellowstone" series turned people's attention to the cowboy way again. The downtown rodeo parade successfully resumed, and several wagon trains now converge in Montgomery for the rodeo. A growing number of new sponsors have been attracted to the show, along with top rodeo stock contractors, performers, and rodeo contestants.

For the first time, the schedule changed from Thursday through Saturday to Friday through Sunday afternoon. There have been a number of sell-out crowds and the entire cost of the rodeo covered before a single ticket was sold. The schedule change also allowed for a Cowboy Church service on Sunday morning, which has been well-attended. I am proud to participate in the service.

Things are really looking up for the SLE! My brother, Linwood will be the President of the SLE in 2025, which is very special to me. I hope the old rodeo continues to survive and thrive.

I now live in Weatherford, Texas and am a Parker County Sheriff's Posse member. We sponsor both the PRCA rodeo and Ranch rodeo here. I've been to the Ft. Worth Stock Show and Rodeo, the San Antonio Rodeo, the Working Cowboy Ranch Finals rodeo in Amarillo, the NFR both in Ft. Worth and Las Vegas, and to the daddy of 'em all, Frontier Days in Cheyenne, Wyoming. I've been to many rodeos, small and large, near and far.

Though the years have been swift and the rodeos have been many, I can still see myself as a wide-eyed child leaning as hard as I could across the railing to touch Rowdy Yates' hand when he rode by at the SLE. That home town rodeo shaped me and I'm grateful for the memories.

The past is what God uses to shape us into the people we are today. It can't be re-lived except in memory but no matter what happens now or next, it's something God will use for His glory and our good. God bless the rodeo. God bless the SLE.

~~~~~~~~~~~~~~~~~~~~~~~~~
~~~~~~~~~~~~~~~~~~~~~~~~~

"HOMETOWN RODEO"

They took me to the rodeo,
When I was just a kid,
The sights and sounds and pageantry,
I'm glad that's what they did.

The horses, cattle, cowboys,
The flags and cheering crowd,
The ropin' and the ridin',
Everybody clappin' loud.

And sometimes the stars would come,
Roy and Dale and Clint,
Festus and Miss Kitty,
So many of them sent.

And to me it seemed unreal,
'Cause after it was through,
We'd go home back to the ranch,
And do what cowboys do.

So life was in the shadow,
Of our rodeo each year,
And I looked forward to it,
And never had a fear,

That there would ever come a day,
When the rodeo was through,
And though there were some lean years,
It's something they still do.

And later I'll load horses,
From Texas hit the road,
And head to Alabama,
Where I have always showed,

That I love that rodeo,
Where friends and family meet,
I can't wait to see 'em all,
A horseback there to greet.

It's time for home town rodeo,
And I'm soon on the way,
We'll cowboy up and have some fun,
Thankful to rodeo today!

And this year we will praise the Lord,
At Cowboy Church and all,
Point each one to Jesus,
And on Him they can call.

~~~~~~~~~~~~~~~~~~~~~~~~~
~~~~~~~~~~~~~~~~~~~~~~~~~

"And whatever you do or say, do it as a representative of the Lord Jesus, giving thanks through Him to God the Father..."
Colossians 4:17, NLT

Whatever we do or say...that's a tall order! But Paul's counsel is that all be done with a view toward representing Jesus well. Maybe the Lord is speaking to you about your work or place of employment, and how you represent Him there. Perhaps the Lord is dealing with you about how you represent Him to members of your immediate family. Maybe, like our rodeo, you're attending a special, annual event with friends and family. How shall we represent Jesus there? It makes all of life a mission, and all about Jesus, no matter the particulars. Whatever you do or say...

Prayer Starter: Lord, help me to represent You well,

____

____

____

____

____

____

____

____

___________________ in Jesus' name.

DOUBLE-HOCKED MY DADDY

I caught the roping virus when I was twelve years old, and never got over it. The year was1964, and my hero was Dean Oliver, who won eight world championships between 1956 and 1969 in tie-down calf roping. I had a rope in my hand as long as I can remember, but when I turned twelve, Dad gave me a rope horse for my birthday, a pretty dun I named Dizzy.

I spent most of my time roping. I was either calf roping in the arena, roping to doctor yearlings in the pasture, or catching escapees from the lease pastures. Dad wasn't a roper, nor did he love horses. Dad felt that horses were the necessary tools of the trade and he never kept one that wouldn't behave. If Dad bought a horse, he bought it to work.

If any of the ranch horses bucked or caused any kind of problem, he sold 'em. In his mind there was too much work to do to fool with one that wouldn't load, or stand for the farrier, or was hard-mouthed, or pitched, or you couldn't use to rope a yearling. It's just the way it was. As a result we rode good horses and you could rope off of any of them. So, when Dad bought Dizzy, I finally had my own and I stayed after it.

Watching the cowboys who were employed by my Dad made me want to be a good roper. Back then we knew nothing about dally roping. I didn't even know it existed. Every rope was tied on hard and fast to the saddle horn. The longest ropes were about thirty-five feet long, most closer to thirty, and there were only two kinds: manila and nylon.

The old manila or grass ropes were better for roping calves or small cattle because they were more limber. You could get your slack quicker with them. The problem with those ropes was if they got wet or cold they became as stiff as a cable. I've known a manila rope to break, and usually at a very inconvenient time. You had to find a way to dry 'em out to get them limber enough to use effectively. Sometimes we put 'em under the hood of a cranked pickup truck to dry up or warm up. Kids now a days wouldn't understand.

The advantage of using a nylon rope was that you couldn't break one. The disadvantage was that they were heavy and very stiff when you bought 'em. Back in my day, there was no such thing as a "soft lay." I remember we would attach a new nylon rope to a tree or a stout fence post and then tie the other end to a trailer hitch on the back of a pickup truck. We would leave it that way to stretch it for several days before we used it. As it aged, it became more and more limber and fuzzier, and was a prized possession.

Working cattle, the only time we needed to throw a heel loop was when we were in the pasture doctoring yearlings. Back then there was no team roping for us, only tie-down calf roping. Sometimes we needed to heel one that had gotten out, so we could make the head catch into a halter and drag 'em onto a trailer. But when we were checking cattle and saw a sick one, the first cowboy who could, got a rope on the animal's head or horns. The other would rope the heels and we'd stretch 'em out and give 'em a shot from the saddle bags.

I loved stretching out the yearlings and thought it was absolutely the best, so I practiced that heel throw over and over, trying to make sure that the nylon stood up so the heels could be caught. I roped at pretty much anything that moved- dogs, cats, ducks, goats, whatever- and constantly practiced by roping a five-gallon feed bucket. They kidded me about even sleeping with my rope in my hand.

One fall Saturday morning, after we had been sorting cattle, I grabbed my nylon rope from the fence post and walked toward the house from the barn. It was almost time for lunch, which we called dinner in those days. I swung my loop over my head as I walked, and got to one of my favorite spots to rope a bucket.

The bucket was sitting right where I left it beside the fence. There was a cattle truck and trailer parked nearby so I started practicing over to the side of it. I counted five throws in a row without missing, and then I saw Dad, walking from the barn.

He always walked quickly, always had something to do and somewhere to go. He had a sheaf of cattle bills in his hand and a cattle whip under his arm. He was was wearing a light blue work shirt, a straw cowboy hat, and khakis hooked over the top of his boots. He was looking down at the paperwork as he walked toward me. Something came over me and I decided to rope Dad.

I moved over behind the cattle trailer where he couldn't see me. As he approached, I slowly twirled my rope. My heart began to beat fast. My mind raced and my hands got sweaty. I really didn't want to miss, but I wasn't sure I wanted to catch him either. When Dad was almost even with the end of the trailer, still looking down at his cattle bills, I made my throw.

With one swift toss, I laid a perfect heel loop right at his feet! He walked right into it and I lifted the slack. The loop tightened just below his knees and I gave it a little jerk. Dad stumbled and the cattle bills flew up in the air. I threw down the rope and ran.

Dad righted himself and looked around to see what had happened. As I ran out of sight, he shouted, "Damn, boy!". He didn't follow and I thanked God Dad didn't come after me. Instead, he untangled himself, picked up the cattle papers, and walked on toward the house.

I knew he was going to look at some cattle that afternoon, so I waited outside till his car was gone before I went inside. When Mom saw me come through the door, she laughed and said, "I hear you roped your father."

"Yes ma'am, I did. I caught him by both feet!". Mama smiled.

"What did he say?" I asked.

She laughed. "He said you were really learning to rope."

I felt very relieved because I was expecting a whippin'.

Many years have come and gone since those days. I calf roped for several of those years, and entered the little jackpots for $6, even before I had a driver's license. Sid, our foreman, would take me to the arena and he would rope, too. My old friend, Bruce Brannen, always came around to collect the money and I was proud to give it to him.

I don't know how many cattle I have roped through the years but there were many. I've even dragged calves to the branding fire a few times. I team roped quite a bit, as well as the normal ranch roping. I often team roped with my brother Linwood and my good friend Mark. Though I never considered myself a great roper, I spun lots of loops and made lots of memories.

In it all and through it all, the memory I'll never forget is that perfect heel loop I threw when I double-hocked my Daddy, and Daddy gave me grace.

~~~~~~~~~~~~~~~~~~~~~~~~~~

"Be gentle and ready to forgive; never hold grudges. Remember, the Lord forgave you, so you must forgive others."
Colossians 3:13 (TLB)
~~~~~~~~~~~~~~~~~~~~~~~~~~

"DOUBLE-HOCKED MY DADDY"

___

I was ropin' that old bucket,
Was maybe twelve years old,
Throw and catch and throw again,
To practice hours untold.

And along came my old Daddy,
And he was walkin' fast,
Was lookin' down at cow bills,
I knew he'd soon walk past.

I stood behind a cattle truck,
And slowly twirled my rope,
Decided I'd catch Daddy,
At least that was my hope.

And then before you know it,
I laid a heel loop down,
And double-hocked my Daddy,
Without a single sound.

One little jerk, he stumbled,
Threw down my rope and ran,
It wasn't Bible language,
Those words of his weren't bland.

But I did not wait for him,
I just ran and hid,
Waited till he drove away,
'Fore tellin' Momma what I did.

She only laughed a little,
But said we'd wait and see,
When home from the cow sale,
Learn what he'd do to me.

And later on that evenin',
The look on my Dad's face,
Let me know I'd get some,
Unexpected grace.

The Good Lord will surprise you,
With a special dose of grace,
And you know you don't deserve it,
But it helps you run life's race.

And I'll not forget the moment,
A long, long time ago,
When I double-hocked my Daddy,
And grace was what he showed.

"He forgave us all our sins, having canceled the written code, with its regulations, that was against us and that stood opposed to us; He took it away, nailing it to the cross…"
Colossians 2:13-14, NIV

Being forgiven is a miracle of grace. It's startling, surprising, and overwhelmingly generous. All sins forgiven and never brought up again. Debt canceled, disobedience pardoned, guilt absolved, penalty removed. Forgotten forever…period. Done deal. Have you been surprised by His forgiveness? Or the grace that comes when He calls you to do something you can't do? And then you can because He empowers you. Or the grace that helps you overcome something that would otherwise do you in or make you give up altogether? But you don't because somehow His grace is sufficient and makes your weakness strong.

As my friend, Dr. Stan Cobb, recently told me, "Grace always surprises me!" Or as Phillips, Craig, and Dean sing, "his grace still amazes me…". Amazing and surprising and almost too wonderful to be true. But it is.

Prayer Starter: Lord, help me receive and freely share Your surprising grace,

____

____

____

____

____in Jesus' name.

BIG CATTLE

It was the fall of the year and I was twelve years old. We were gathering steers, about a thousand of them, that had been turned out on native pasture for a year. They would soon be shipped out to the feed lots in Texas or other places. They were mostly cross-bred cattle that had come from Florida as yearling bulls weighing three to four hundred pounds. They now weighed more than twice that and some weighed well over nine hundred pounds. Penning them was a chore because they were spread out in several lease pastures over two counties and lots of them were wild. Invariably some would get away and had to be roped.

Though I had a rope in my hand most of the time and had been roping calves in the arena and roping and doctoring yearlings for over a year, Dad felt it was too dangerous for me to help go after those big wild cattle. He figured it could be dangerous and he was afraid I would get hurt.

One week we were gathering some of these steers when we learned that two or three of them were in a neighbor's pasture across the highway. We went to get 'em and it took all morning to push 'em out of the brush, even with dogs. When they finally came out of the woods everybody took a shot. One of the steers was caught immediately but the second one dodged every loop. Three in a row missed and he was headed back to the woods when I caught him. He was a big, old red steer that weighed at least nine hundred, the first big one I ever caught. "Don't say anything to your Dad," Sid told me, "and we won't, either." I didn't and neither did they. But I was very excited. The cowboys, my heroes, had seen me do what they did. It felt good.

The next week we saddled in the dark and hauled the horses to another rent pasture that had about a hundred fifty steers. We were sitting horseback when the sun came up and we had most of the steers penned by 10:00 A.M. Sid said he thought he had seen a little bunch that we missed, and when we made a second circle, we jumped two big steers. One was a Hereford cross and another was light-colored and looked like he was mostly charbray.

The Hereford steer turned toward the catch pen and went on, but the charbray tried to escape us. Every cowboy- Sid, Dean, Billy and R.C. rode up, roped and missed. I took a shot just as he hit the woods and missed, too. But I followed him, limbs popping, and rebuilt my loop as we ran. My good buck-skin horse, Dizzy, stayed right on him, and when we hit a clearing, I dabbed my loop right on him. Everyone else came up whooping and hollering and said I was going to need a bigger hat 'cause I was going to get a big head.

Weeks passed and we kept gathering and doing what we always did. One day when we were saddling our horses, Dad yelled out, "Don't let Brad rope any of these big cattle." He told it to our foreman, Sidney Joe Davis, and the others, Dean and Bill and R.C. They all nodded seriously and said, "Yessir." But it had already happened, you see, but they didn't let on. I didn't, either.

I've thrown many a loop since then, both in the pasture and in life. I've missed many times. I have been so discouraged at times I refused to throw a loop. Truth is, you miss a hundred per cent of the throws you never make. It's important to keep on, to learn from every miss and celebrate every catch. Galatians 6:9 tells us "Let us not become weary in doing good, for at the proper time we will reap a harvest if we do not give up". By the grace of God, I am learning to stand up in the stirrups and keep on trying.

"BOYS TO MEN"

Yes, they call 'em cowboys,
But they aren't boys at all,
Unless you say they're good old boys,
And that's a sometimes call.

'Cause see it's been a long time,
Since boys is what they are,
Although they like to laugh and play,
They act like men, by far.

They've learned to keep their promise,
To stand by what they say,
Boys still like to change their minds,
And will from day to day.

Men get up and go to work,
Boys, they call in sick,
If you're in trouble, need some help,
A man will show up quick.

A boy will use a woman,
A man knows how to love,
A boy still just promotes himself,
Men point to God above.

A man knows when to shut his mouth,
A boy will jabber on,
A man respects a better hand,
A boy thinks he alone,

Knows more than the oldsters,
That's why he's hard to bear,
He'll often rush the cattle,
You'd best not have him there.

'Cause he'll react when he is told,
Instead of watch and learn,
From men who know because their years,
Earned for them their turn.

Boys, they say, will yet be boys,
But with God's grace and aid,
They can change and become men,
'Cause men aren't born, they're made.

And those of us with tired hands,
Comes time to pass the rope,
We've seen some boys that we can trust,
And they give us the hope,

That what we know will live through them,
As they become God's men,
Cowboys by the grace of God,
But those who trust in Him.

~~~~~~~~~~~~~~~~~~~~~~~~~

"Be on guard. Stand firm in the faith. Be courageous. Be strong. And do everything with love."
1 Corinthians 16:13-14 (NLT)

The old King James translation of this verse says: "Quit ye like men. Be strong." In other words, "man up!" It's all about having the God-given courage to take responsibility and do the right thing. It's not for the timid or immature. It's for those who are willing to step up in faith and live a life of radical, God-breathed love. Cowards become heroes. Failures become leaders. Boys become men. And it's all by the grace of God.

Prayer Starter: Lord, help me stand firm and do everything with love,

____

____

____

____

____

____

—

in Jesus' name.
~~~~~~~~~~~~~~~~~~~~~~~~~

DEAD OR ALIVE

I was on my way to the barn when I saw her coming straight toward me. A cow jumped out of one of the lots adjoining the barn and came barreling down the lane that led to the house. She weighed close to a thousand pounds and was a big ole Brangus. I made some noise and flapped my arms a time or two, but she only got faster. I went for the fence and she blew past me with a snort. "No problem," I thought to myself. "She'll stop when she gets to the gate that was firmly chained shut." The gate itself was imposing, five and a half feet tall, made of welded pipe and with heavy, welded wire mesh from top to bottom, end to end. There was no getting past that gate, so I thought. I was wrong.

When she got to the gate she never broke stride. She leaped like a deer, got her front quarters over the top, and did a complete somersault over it, landing on her back on the other side. The top pipe of the gate was bent down into a "v" where she hit it and went over. She then scrambled to her feet, and took off running again, straight out the long driveway that led to the bypass. She crossed four lanes of interstate, including a wide median, and jumped the fence on the other side. She didn't stop there. She crossed a hundred and fifty acres in a matter of minutes, entered the woods on the far side, and jumped the back fence into the Gunter Air Force Base property. High headed ole' heifer.

Dad wasn't happy when i told him what happened. "I want y'all to find that cow, catch her, and bring her back over here," he'd say.

Every cowboy on the ranch, including myself would answer with a loud, "Yessir." But we never could. Occasionally we would see her, but never could get to her before she'd break for high ground.

About four months after her grand escape, Sid, our ranch foreman and I were headed home after a long day of checking cattle. Our saddled horses were loaded behind us in the stock trailer we were pulling. As we traveled the interstate that divided our property, Sid said, "Look yonder! There's that old cow that got out a few months ago!" I looked where he pointed and sure enough, there she was, grazing in a long, open pasture on the far side of the highway. "Let's go get her!" he said.

My heart began to race. We got turned around and pulled into the driveway that led to the gate opening into what we called the "new ground" pasture.

We got the horses unloaded as quickly and quietly as possible, tightened our cinches, and stepped into the saddle. We rode out of the catch pen and through a small stand of trees on the other side, building our loops. As we came into the open, the cow threw up her head and saw us. She was about a hundred yards away, and took off running with her tail in the air. "Here we go!" Sid hollered, and away we went.

Galloping full speed, Sid got the cow lined out and his bay horse, Waxy, tracked her like white on rice. Waxy was a cow horse Dad bought from a customer in Waxahachie, Texas, and he was a good one. Sid threw his lariat rope and the loop landed on top of her head (she had no horns) but never dropped all the way down so he could pull his slack. The bottom of the rope hung across the the top of her nose, and Sid must have fished that loop down for a couple hundred feet. Finally, he snatched if off, and shouted for me to catch her.

I was galloping along behind Sid, and by now the cow had slowed down a little. I was thirteen years old and had been roping calves and yearlings for about a year. I knew if I missed she probably would escape into the woods and be gone again.

I tossed my rope and caught her, as pretty as you please. My good dun horse, Dizzy, shut it down just like when we roped a calf, and when she hit the end of the rope she started bellowing and pulling him along. We were tied on hard and fast. Sid came galloping up swinging his rope to get another loop on her and just as he got close, his girth broke and his saddle slipped to the side. He hit the ground so hard it brought tears to my eyes, and he crawled around on all fours for a few minutes trying to recover his senses.

By then the cow had turned and was fighting my horse. He side-stepped her, but I barely avoided getting the rope hung up under him. She stood there panting, and Sid finally stood up, walked over and said, "Give me your horse and I'll hold the cow while you go back for the truck." He stepped on my horse, and I pulled the saddle off his horse and trotted him bareback to the truck. I tied his horse and cranked it, then headed out across the pasture, pulling the trailer behind.

When I got back to Sid and the cow, I stopped and threw the trailer gate open. He got her circled around and pulled her to the door of the trailer. So far, so good, but then she balked, choked down, and fell over. Sid jumped off my horse and ran to the cow. He loosened the rope from her neck and started pumping on her side. But it was too late. She was dead.

Sid looked at me and said, "I'm gonna stick her, and you stay here while I take the horses back. I'll send you some help, and y'all get this cow cut up." He pulled out his Case pocket-knife and cut her throat. Then he loaded my horse and his saddle, stopped at the gate for his horse, and I watched him drive away.

Sitting on the grass beside a dead cow was a new experience. The day was growing dark and dusk was settling on the pastures. After what seemed forever, I finally saw headlights piercing the black sky as a pick up truck bounced across the pasture towards me. It was Henry, one of the men who worked for Dad. I was very glad to see him. "I see y'all got dat cow," he said.

"Yessir, we got her, all right, and I'm sure glad you came to help me." I was relieved, to tell the truth. Nighttime in the pastures was full of sounds and critters.

"We'll see about her," he said. Working with the headlights shining on us, we field-dressed and gutted the cow. He then took a hack saw and while I held onto what I could, he got her cut up into four quarters. We put all four in the back of his truck, and left everything else for the varmints and buzzards. They had a feast, I'm sure.

I climbed into Henry's old truck and we drove back across the pastures to our ranch house. No one was home to tell us otherwise, so we unloaded the four quarters and placed each one on a wrought iron lawn chair on Mom's back patio. Henry told me good night and went on home.

I was still standing at the back porch by myself, hosing the grass and dirt off the fresh beef when Dad and Mom drove up about thirty minutes later. I can't imagine what Mama must of thought. Dad got out and immediately wanted to know what I was doing. "What's all this?" He asked.

"You remember that old Brangus cow that got out about four months ago? I said. "Well, here she is. We got her back."

He just stood there and laughed for a minute. Then he said, 'Well, I didn't say I wanted y'all to get her back dead or alive, but I'm glad you got her." Dad hung the quarters in the cooler, and it wasn't long before we went on to bed. I was tired, but it took me a long time to unwind that night and get to sleep.

When I think of that moment, so very long ago, I'm reminded that God is always after us when we run away and go jumping fences where we don't belong. He always comes after us. He's got a long rope and a fast horse. There's a difference here. He wants us alive, not dead... And that's a good thing to remember.

~~~~~~~~~~~~~~~~~~~~~~~~~

~~~~~~~~~~~~~~~~~~~~~~~~~

"ONCE UPON A COWBOY TIME"

Once upon a cowboy time,
We rode the range so free,
It was so very long ago,
All my old pards and me.

We chased the bovine cross the plains,
We roped 'em when we could,
We helped each other everyday,
And showed our friends we would.

The cow boss always led the way,
No gunsel got ahead,
And if he did he paid the price,
By all the grief we fed.

We went to town 'bout once a month,
We drank till cash ran out,
We slowly rode back to the ranch,
And said no more, no doubt.

One day a preacher traveled by,
He shared the Lord's Good News,
Right from the Good Book clear he read,
And said Christ paid our dues.

I was touched by what he preached,
I heard it as a child,
But I had never prayed that prayer,
And now a cowboy wild,

I thought it was too late for me,
To ever change my ways,
But he said no, that I should ask,
For grace that comes and stays.

And so I got down on my knees,
And prayed the sinner's prayer,
Lord, forgive me, come on in,
He saved me then and there.

And all the cowboys, one by one,
Came to do the same,
The Holy Spirit did His work,
They called on Jesus' name.

Except for our old cow boss,
He said it's not for me,
And though we prayed and hoped he would,
Refused till finally,

We were bringing in some bulls,
And some were bad to fight,
And as we pushed 'em all along,
We saw an awful sight.

This old bull had downed his horse,
And pinned him to the ground,
Laying there was all broke up,
What we rode up and found.

Boys, he said, I'm glad you came,
But it's too late for me,
I'll soon be gone, please say a prayer,
For I'm hell-bound, you see.

I said no, it's not too late,
If you will call on Him,
He bowed his head and gave his heart,
Before death did him in.

All this happened long ago,
I write it now for you,
'Cause if you do not know the Lord,
It's not too late, it's true.

Just bow your heart and call on Him,
To forgive your every sin,
And Jesus Christ who died and rose,
Will surely come right in.

~~~~~~~~~~~~~~~~~~~~~~~~
~~~~~~~~~~~~~~~~~~~~~~~~

"Everyone who calls on the name of the Lord will be saved..."
Romans 10:13 (NIV)

Calling on the name of the Lord means I intentionally pray and ask the Lord to do for me what He has promised. I acknowledge that I've sinned and ask His forgiveness. I accept His gift of pardon and ask Him to take control of my life. There is no "sinner's prayer" spelled out in scripture, but calling on Him embodies these basic components. One may not fully understand salvation when they call on the Lord. They may have a very elemental understanding of God's grace as offered through the death and resurrection of Jesus. But one does not have to be theologically astute to be saved. We just have to call on Him to do it for us. I've known people who simply prayed, "Lord, have mercy," who received salvation and their life changed. If you are not sure you've called on Him, then now would be a good time to do it, and ask Him to make you sure it has happened.

Lord, help make me sure that I have received salvation...

____

____

____

____

____

____

__________, in Jesus' name.

HIPPIE

Anti-Viet Nam war protests frequently made headlines and America had 500,000 troops deployed. Batman was the new TV show, and Star Trek began that fall. It was the spring of the year, and we had already had the SLE rodeo in March out at the Coliseum. The year was 1966 and I was fourteen years old.

It was a Thursday afternoon and Dad called to say me and Billy Carter should load one of our yearlings on the stock trailer and haul him out to the stockyards. Sale day was every Friday at the old Capitol Stockyards in Montgomery, Alabama, and dad wanted the steer to get to the Friday sale. I can't remember exactly why Dad wanted to sell this yearling. Maybe he was a chronic we couldn't get straightened out, but I'm not sure.

I was always excited to go anywhere with Billy. He had worked for Dad for a couple years, was soft-spoken, and had a distinctive cowboy style. He was the first I ever knew to wear big rowel spurs. When he rode the good, gray gelding he called Badger, he tapped those rowels on the back girth as he went. It was something I noticed.

We spent a lot of time together, riding pastures, doctoring yearlings, fixing fences, or whatever we were sent to do. I remember the day Billy took his plug tobacco from his front pocket and cut off a chew with his pocketknife. I asked for some. He chuckled as he cut me off a piece, then said, "Just be sure to spit or it'll make you sick." I spit and it worked out okay. I didn't get sick, but sometimes now I wish I had.

On this particular Thursday Billy was in no hurry. That's another thing I liked about him. With Dad you could never do things fast enough, but not Billy. He traveled steady but never rushed. He always took his time- with cattle, with horses, and with an impressionable boy like me. He always made me feel accepted and especially when I asked him questions. That wasn't something I could do with Dad.

We got the calf unloaded and Billy got the paperwork from the stockyard hand to give to Dad later. The shadows were lengthening when we pulled out of the parking lot of the Capitol, and headed back to the ranch. Billy asked me if I was hungry. I said, "I sure am," and we pulled over at a little diner style café with a long lunch counter with stools and a couple of booths on the other side. There used to be lots of places like this, and we sat side by side on the stools and looked at the menu.

The diner wasn't very big and there was only one waitress. We were the only customers. I remember the waitress because she had dyed her hair an unusual shade of red and she had red fingernail polish to match. "What are you cowboys going to have today?" she asked. Billy ordered a cup of coffee and a piece of apple pie. I asked for a slice of coconut cream pie with a coke. She jotted down our order, winked at Billy, and walked away.

While we waited, a fellow came in and sat at the other end of the lunch counter. He had long, blonde hair that fell to his shoulders. He wore a tee shirt with jeans and he had on sandals. I watched him walk across the room. I noticed he had a string of love beads around his neck. He nodded to Billy and Billy nodded back.

At first, the waitress acted like she didn't see the guy, and when she finally acknowledged him, she was decidedly unfriendly. He smiled and ordered a cup of coffee. Billy and I got our pie and ate quietly, not saying much at all. After Billy finished his coffee, he paid the bill and we got in the truck and headed home.

After a mile or two I broke into conversation. In an effort to sound grown-up, I laughed and asked Billy what he thought about that hippie's long hair. "He looked like a girl," I said. There was a long moment of silence in the truck, and then Billy leaned forward and turned down the volume on the radio. I can't be for sure, but I think the song was "Hey Good Lookin'" by Hank, Sr. Then Billy said something I never forgot.

"You know, Brad, that young fella didn't laugh at my cowboy hat. So, I'm not going to laugh at his long hair." I didn't know what to say… my Dad had lots of negative things to say about hippies. They were dirty trouble-makers as far as Dad was concerned. I assumed Billy Carter felt the same way. I was wrong.

It's been a long time since 1966. As far as I knew, Billy Carter wasn't much of a church-goer. He chewed Bull of the Woods and smoked Picayune cigarettes. He'd occasionally drink a cold beer. But when it came to treating other human beings the way he wanted to be treated, his behavior was right on target. We can learn from men like Billy Carter, those who are rich in spirit despite their appearance. Matthew 7:12 (ESV) says, " So *whatever you wish that others would do to you, do also to them...*", Billy did just that. We should all aspire to be so.

~~~~~~~~~~~~~~~~~~~~~~~~~~

"Therefore, whenever we have the opportunity, we should do good to everyone-especially to those in the family of faith." **Galatians 6:10 (NLT)**

"But the fruit of the Spirit is love, joy, peace, forbearance, kindness, goodness, faithfulness, gentleness and self-control. Against such things there is no law."
Galatians 5:22-23 (NIV)
~~~~~~~~~~~~~~~~~~~~~~~~~~

"HIPPIE"

We had just unloaded cattle,
At the stockyard across town,
We pulled into a parking lot,
Went in and sat down,

On stools 'longside a counter,
With one short-order cook,
A kindly little waitress,
Who soon our order took.

It was me and Billy Carter,
And I was just a kid,
Billy wore his big rowel spurs,
Just like he always did.

He got a piece of apple pie,
With coffee hot and black,
And me I ordered ice cold coke,
And some French fries in a sack.

Then, as we were eating,
A fellow walked inside,
A tee shirt and bell bottom jeans,
Couldn't miss him if you tried.

Clear he was a hippie,
His hair was shoulder-length,
Back then it was unusual,
The waitress gave a wink.

But soon our break was over,
Climbed in the truck and gone,
I laughed when I asked Billy,
'Bout the hippie's hair so long.

He seemed like a nice person,
Was all that old Bill said,
And then he simply added,
Tipped his hat back on his head,

That guy, he was a hippie,
And the difference plain to see,
But I will not make fun of him,
He didn't laugh at me.

He could've mocked my spurs and boots,
Or, yes, my cowboy hat,
Instead he smiled and nodded,
His manners were like that.

I never did forget it,
Though I always tried to be,
Just like Billy Carter,
Who was cowboy to a T.

When he praised that hippie's manners,
He knew much more than me,
'Bout how we should treat people,
And how things ought to be.

Let's try to help each other,
Not tear each other down,
Specially when they're different,
And want to come around.

~~~~~~~~~~~~~~~~~~~~~~~~
~~~~~~~~~~~~~~~~~~~~~~~~

"...since God loved us that much, we surely ought to love each another..."
1 John 4:11 (NLT)

According to scripture, it's nonsense to say we love God whom we can't see, when we don't love people whom we can see. Love for God and love for others cannot be separated. They go together. God loved us first and we show we've received it by giving it away. We become a catalyst for His love. Another way to say it is if we truly love God, the world will get the overflow. This all breaks down when we allow the way people look or act to affect our love for them. When we see them the way God does, this breakdown will be healed, and God's love will be brought to full expression in us.

Prayer Starter: Lord, teach me to love others the way You have loved me,

____

____

____

____

______in Jesus' name.

MENDIN' FENCES

One of my earliest memories was being sent to do fence repair. Dad would say, "Saddle your horse, Brad, and go down there where the cattle are getting out and fix it." I'd go catch my horse and then get a bucket of feed and toll him in from the lot where we kept eight to ten usin' horses. I'd slip the halter on him and lead him out in front of the saddle room, then brush him down and throw my old Billy Cook on him. I loved that saddle. I got it from Jimmy Alverson at the Montgomery Serum Company when I was twelve years old.

After tightening my cinch, I strapped saddle bags behind the saddle and put staples and a fence hammer inside, along with a small bundle of foot long pieces of barbless wire that had been cut off a coil.

I always knew about where the repair was needed. I'd find the place, get off and tie my horse, and get to work. Sometimes the wire was stretched and saggy and just needed to be re-stapled to the post and stretched tight. Sometimes it was broken completely , in which case I used the shorter pieces to pull it back together. If it was too bad, I'd patch it as best I could and let somebody know it needed more work. I couldn't do much if the post was broken, and sometimes it was.

Fence work was mean work- hot in the summertime and cold in the winter. The mosquitos would drive you crazy when the weather was warm, and the sweat was dripping off your hat brim. Seemed like there was always a place in the fence to mend.

The hardest part was not the wire or the heat or the cold or the mosquitos. No, the hard part happened when Dad came to see the place I had fixed. He'd look at it and groan as he shook his head. Then he'd say, "This is the nearest nothing I've ever seen," followed by, "how could you have been stupid enough to do it this way."

I didn't say much when Dad evaluated my fence work. When he was really uptight, he'd demand an answer. I would say, "I don't know."

"You've gotta know, son." After he fixed it the way he wanted it done, it looked pretty much the same to me, so I never quite figured out what he wanted. I sure spent a lot of time trying to get it right, though!

Back in those days Dad leased a lot of country. These pastures were scattered all around our area, and yearlings were turned out on each one. There was one on Norman Bridge Road, one on Taylor Road in Cecil, Alabama, and the largest way down near Lowndesboro.

Dad didn't believe in spending much money on fences, so there was a continuous need for repair. A storm would blow down a tree limb on the fence and the cattle would escape. They were mostly crossbred, Florida cattle that came through the sale barn, so all of them were wild and crazy anyhow. A good fence wouldn't hold some of 'em, but let a tree limb fall in one place on several miles of fence and they'd find the hole.

I always wondered where the cattle thought they were going. Sometimes they got out where there was a creek running through the pasture and fence was built across it to keep the cattle in. If the creek flooded, sometimes the fence would wash away entirely. If it got dry and the creek got low, the cattle could walk out under the fence. It was always something to keep a water gap fixed.

One time I was talking to Mama and said, "Mom, I know about Angus, Hereford, Brahma, Charolais, Santa Gertrudis, Shorthorn, and lots more. But Mama, what kind of cow is a 'bitch'?"

She laughed and said, "Oh, honey, that's not a breed. That's what your Dad calls the ones that get out."

Most of my memories revolve around times I fixed fences alone but I also worked alongside fence fixers, too. Sidney Joe Davis, Dad's ranch foreman, could work magic when it came to patching and stretching wire. He taught me how to use a green bodock limb to twist and stretch wire tight.

Another hand, R.C. Holten, stayed cleaner than any of the others while working on a fence or anything else. He was a deputy sheriff and did day work for us. One time we were pulling wire on a hot day and he sent me to his truck for water. There was a mason jar full of water on his front seat beside his thermos, but when I unscrewed the top, I knew real quick that it wasn't water. It was white lightning! I put the lid on as fast as I could and grabbed the thermos. When I got back to R. C., he asked, "You didn't open that mason jar, did you?"

"No sir." I lied.

The last time I saw R. C. Holten alive on this earth, I was driving down Wasden Road in Lowndes County and I looked across a pasture to see a fence crew setting posts and pulling wire. R.C. threw up his hand as we drove by.

One of the features of leased ranch fencing is what we call gaps. These were exit and entry places, usually in a corner, where you moved cattle through. It was made of wire and smaller posts, and when closed was stretched across the space. The fence post that held it in place had a piece of wire stapled at the top and the bottom that made a little circle of wire.

The gap was designed so that the end post of the gate part had to be stuck into the two little circles of wire. You had to put the bottom of the post in first, then pull the top as hard as you could and fasten it in place. I know this description probably doesn't make sense to someone who's never had to open or close one, but suffice to say they could be difficult. They had to be fixed sometimes, too.

I grew up fixing fences at home and the fences were many. Linwood and I worked on fences a lot. One time we were working in a hot, tight, brushy place with lots of briars and thorns. The mosquitos were about to carry us off, and in an effort to get the wire stretched I managed to thoroughly bend my hat brim on a tree limb. He looked at me and said, in a gravelly voice, "We got us the Josey Wales." It was darn funny at the time.

Time passed and our old home place was lost. Later, however, Dad bought four hundred acres of good pastureland. One of the things I appreciated the most was that we built good fences at the new place. I was grown by the time it happened, but no matter. It made me proud. I thought, "I'll never have to fool with those raggedy fences again."

Dad being Dad, later decided he needed to lease some pasture. He leased in places like Ada and Sprague, Alabama to name a couple of them. Guess what? The fences needed fixing!

He turned out about four hundred head at home and then another four hundred on the lease. "Brad," he'd say, "you and Linwood go down there and find the place where the cattle are getting out. Y'all do your best to get the fence fixed."

Sound familiar?

We'd go do our best to mend the fence, over and over again. I can't talk about mending fences without talking about digging post holes with hole-diggers, which is unforgiving work. If it's dry and the ground is hard, you hope you can auger it out before you dig by hand. If it's wet, that old mud is so slick it sticks to everything. They say if you stick to the prairie when it's dry, it'll stick to you when it's wet.

I've said many o' time that the devil has used fence work to teach cowboys new curse words. The real bad words are learned when you're stretchin' gaucho barbed wire. It's light gaged and the barbs are extra sharp. Without gloves, forget trying to use it. Getting holes dug and stretching gaucho wire has sent more than one cowboy to the city limits to find a town job.

In 2021, when Stacey and I bought our little place in Weatherford, Texas, I knew I'd be fencin' again. No one had ever lived on it so almost everything had to be done from scratch, including the driveway. Part of my ongoing task is to build fences and keep them repaired. I build fences to keep the cattle in. I build fences to keep the predators out. I build and I repair the boundaries of my home. Every post, every stretch of wire reminds me of where I've come from and where I'm going. Every day that I stretch wire, I think of Dad. He would have liked it here.

Lately I often think about my old friend, Mark Eagerton. Mark was a master fence builder. He got too hot one summer day in the Alabama heat and he collapsed. He never regained consciousness and then died a week later. The memory of his death reminds me that fence building can be lethal. No matter the struggles, no matter the heat nor the endless hours, however, fences must be tended to.

Dad's been in heaven now since 2001 and sometimes I can still hear his voice telling me to fix the fence. I also hear the Father's voice telling me to tend to my fence, to stand guard at the gap. Especially as a father, a husband, a man, it's my job to watch over the spiritual fences, the invisible fences that serve as boundaries for how we live and behave and who we let in.

Some folks may have forgotten the importance of a good fence. Some have let the devil destroy the fences, and are paying for it in very expensive ways. Some may have never built a fence or set a post. Some may know how, but are out of the habit.

If you've neglected to keep your fence fixed, I pray the Lord helps you see the boundary lines and pick up the hammer and staples and walk the line, mend the holes, close the gap and stretch the wire along the outskirts of life.

~~~~~~~~~~~~~~~~~~~~~~~~

"No longer will violence be heard in your land, nor ruin or destruction within your borders, but you will call your walls Salvation and your gates Praise."
Isaiah 60:18 (NIV)
~~~~~~~~~~~~~~~~~~~~~~~~

"Because he bends down to listen, I will pray as long as I have breath!"
Psalm 116:2 (NLT)

"WORK"

If you want it, go and get it,
That's what my Daddy said,
Get up and go work for it,
There's no future in that bed.

His plan was not so easy,
Some thought it was too much,
'Cause if your eyes were open,
You were doing chores and such.

When I was real little,
I learned my work to do,
The kids who lived in town, y'all,
Didn't know the things I knew.

'Bout horses and the cattle,
And feed and giving shots,
Branding and castrating,
Dehorning, planting crops.

I thought it was unfair then,
'Cause they all got to play,
And I was out there working,
Every single day.

Except of course on Sunday,
'Cause we had church to do,
And sometimes on a Saturday,
Take off to go hunt, too.

You can't really imagine,
How I felt when I,
Heard some felt entitled,
To get things without try.

They thought they should be given,
What was owed to them,
Because their dead ancestors,
Were mistreated way back when.

I couldn't understand it,
And really I still can't,
I've seen folks even riot,
And raise their voice in rant.

And, yes, all men are equal,
And every life has worth,
I believe in freedom,
And justice on this earth.

But seems to me you're equal,
If you have the chance,
To go and make your living,
And free to join the dance.

But if you will not earn it,
Outcome's not guaranteed,
It's just the chance you're given,
And not results, you see.

Revive that old work ethic,
Say it loud and long,
Get up and go work for it,
With that you can't go wrong.

~~~~~~~~~~~~~~~~~~~~~~~~~

"Those unwilling to work will not get to eat..."
2 Thessalonians 3:10 (NLT)

Work is a sacred assignment from God. The benefits of good, hard work are countless. Before sin entered the picture, God tasked Adam and Eve with taking care of the garden. That's the first job mentioned in scripture and it was God-given.

Prayer Starter: Lord, teach me to do my work, thankfully and with integrity,

____

____

____

_________________________________ in Jesus' name.
~~~~~~~~~~~~~~~~~~~~~~~~~

COTTON-EYED JOE

We didn't raise horses when I was growing up. Dad bought ready-to-go-to-work ranch geldings and if they weren't "ready", he'd get rid of them. It wasn't until I was grown that Dad got a handful of brood mares in some real estate deal and we had colts to start. One of the first colts born on our ranch was out of Dad's favorite, a buckskin mare he called Dusty. Dad was not a horse-lover, but he really thought a lot of this mare, and when she had the bay colt he was mighty proud. We named the colt "Cotton-Eyed Joe".

He was a pretty thing. He was a dark bay with only a little sliver of white under his left eye and a white snip on his nose. He was well-built and showed lots of promise. We gelded him as a yearling and halter-broke him by ponying him with the seasoned geldings, then turned him out again. When he was two years old we sacked him out and got a saddle on him. He bucked me off one time, if I remember right, but then became very easy to ride and immediately took to cattle. We were roping yearlings off him just a few weeks later. We figured he was really going to make a horse.

The next time it happened, I was doctoring a yearling in a big bottom near the back of our place. I circled around the steer and could see he was gaunt and off by himself. His eyes and nose were running and needed a shot. I had antibiotic and a syringe in my saddle bag. So Cotton-Eyed Joe tracked him just right and I got the steer roped, but just as I jerked my slack and got my dallies, Joe went to bucking. It was only a couple of jumps, and he didn't buck me off, but then he stopped and didn't do it anymore. He behaved while I gave the calf medicine. I didn't give it much thought.

Weeks passed with quite a lot of time in the saddle, and he acted like a broke horse. Then one day when we had been checking cattle all morning, he did it again. It was a beautiful, sunny fall day about midmorning. We had been riding through cattle for a couple of hours. This time we were walking our horses along slack-reined when, with no warning, Cotton-Eyed Joe broke in two. This time he wasn't so mild.

He went to pitchin' and bucked so hard he pitched me forward onto his neck and finally over his head. When he was done actin' a fool, he stopped and just looked at me. Linwood thought it was funny. I didn't. After I caught my breath, I stepped back on him and rode him around in circle for a while. I spurred him up quite a bit. He was a broke horse again. And so it went.

We decided to do more ground work with Joe, but no matter what we did, we couldn't find any trigger to make him buck. He behaved perfectly, both in the pen and the pasture, so we thought maybe he wouldn't buck anymore. People were already talking about our little bay horse, and how well he watched cattle. He was quick, and very responsive. I was just glad he was over it.

One day we were gathering a pasture with about fifty steers in it. Some people had come out from town to ride with us, and it was going to be a fun day for everybody. Every saddle we had was being used, so I grabbed my old duck-billed Billy Cook. It was the first roping saddle I bought as a kid at the Montgomery Serum Company. The resident cowboy, Jimmy Alverson, sold it to me and I paid $150 for it brand-new. I hadn't ridden the old thing in years, and it had just been sitting there gathering dust in our saddle house on the place. I dusted it off and threw it on Cotton-Eyed Joe.

It was a beautiful day with lots of socializing as we rode. People were laughing and talking, and the gather was relatively easy. We pushed the steers towards a large catch pen that adjoined our barn and other working lots. The fifty steers were pretty cooperative and as we approached the gate, we gave them time to find the opening.

About the time the first ones went in, a couple of yearlings turned toward me as if they were looking for an escape route. I turned them back in the right direction, and Joe behaved perfectly. Then, all of a sudden, he swelled up and started pitching. Somehow the strength of his bucking fit caused both front and back cinches on the old Billy Cook to break. I rode the saddle plumb to the ground and Joe danced to the side and waited for us to catch him.

Some people think there are horses that are what they call "cold-backed." Otherwise gentle, they will sometimes buck when you first get on them. But that was not the pattern of Joe's behavior. We never figured out what made him do it or when he might. All our efforts to make him buck came up empty. He never would.

Dad decided he just wasn't safe enough to keep, and it was hard for me to say otherwise. Dad put the word out that Cotton-Eyed Joe was for sale. Soon a young man drove into our place pulling a one horse trailer behind his pick-up. When he got out, we shook hands. He said he heard that we had a horse for sale. I looked at Linwood and we went and caught Joe.

The young cowboy liked his looks and asked if he could ride him. He pulled a saddle from his truck and put it on Joe. The saddle was a nice, hand-made Wade with bucking rolls and oxbow stirrups. With a fluid motion he caught a handful of mane, turned Joe's head, and stepped on. Cotton-Eyed Joe moved off and did what he was asked to do. He behaved perfectly, and was as pretty as a picture.

I looked at Linwood and he knew what I was thinking. "Are we going to tell him?" I whispered. Linwood nodded yes, and when the young cowboy came back around and stepped off, we knew it was time to tell the rest of the story. We explained that the little bay horse would randomly buck, and that we had never found a trigger or pattern to his behavior. The young cowboy listened attentively, then asked our price for the horse.

Without much haggling the deal was done and we said good-bye to Cotton-Eyed Joe. I've often wondered how long it was before Joe tested that young cowboy. Was it that week or did a month go by before he pulled one of his bucking fits? Maybe the young cowboy was able to figure out more than we did and help Joe stay steady on a permanent basis.

Sometimes I think I can be a lot more like "Cotton-Eyed Joe" than I like to admit. That's because sometimes I do or say something I shouldn't - even though I've been a broke horse a long time. The Lord is still helping me with it. I read the Word daily. I pray. I try to do His will. I try. That's all we can do. 2nd Timothy 3:16 (ESV) says, *"All Scripture is breathed out by God and profitable for teaching, for reproof, for correction, and for training in righteousness,"* If you've been a little cold-backed lately, maybe it's time to dig into the Word.

~~~~~~~~~~~~~~~~~~~~~~~~~~
~~~~~~~~~~~~~~~~~~~~~~~~~~

"STOCKYARD CATTLE"

Jesus called the renegades,
And those fence-jumpers, too,
Might call 'em stockyard cattle,
No pedigrees, it's true.

He gathered all the crazies,
The neglected and abused,
The ones that you could buy dirt cheap,
Fact those are ones He used.

If you looked around His circle,
Prob'ly not a one you'd pick,
To go and change the whole, wide world,
'Cause they couldn't hit a lick.

But when His grace transformed them,
Filled with His Spirit strong,
The very misfits that He chose,
Showed He was never wrong.

A group of no-name nothings,
Without power, wealth, or fame,
Yet it proves to all who care,
The power of Jesus' name.

And in His name they spread the Word,
To people far and near,
And even suffered, gave their lives,
So everyone could hear.

Yes, those old stockyard cattle,
Jesus fed and met their thirst,
And like the Good Book calls it,
The last with Him are first.

~~~~~~~~~~~~~~~~~~~~~~~~~~~
~~~~~~~~~~~~~~~~~~~~~~~~~~~

"But God chose the foolish things of the world to shame the wise; God chose the weak things of the world to shame the strong..."
1 Corinthians 1:27 (NIV)

God is good at choosing people that others would not. Jesus gathered men and women who had significant moral and relational issues and transformed them by His grace. When Paul spread the Good News it was the same way. And so it goes...We are often surprised by the one He uses but we shouldn't be. He proves over and over again that it seems to be His favorite method- to save, fill, and send someone whom others believe is inferior and use them in such a way that only He gets the glory. God always resists the proud, and this is one of the ways He does it- by using the foolish, the weak, the lowly, the despised, and the nothings. In this way He says to us, "Let him who boasts boast in the Lord." Amen.

Prayer Starter: Lord, help me to recognize how You use people whom I would never choose,

____

____

____

____

—

in Jesus' name.

DAD'S GARDEN

I didn't want to write this story, but Stacey insisted. I said, "But it's not a cowboy story." She said, "Yes, but it's country, and people will appreciate it. It's about a place where I spent countless hours as a child and I carry the impact of it to this day. I'm talking about our family garden.

The first family garden was in what used to be an acre-large cattle lot that needed very little fertilizer for obvious reasons. Dad was a big advocate for being as self-sufficient as possible. This not only applied to raising food in the garden, but we also processed one to two steers a year, two hogs, rabbits, and an occasional goat, made venison sausage, and had Nubian milk goats. We had fruit trees, peach, plum and fig, and also a scuppernong arbor.

The garden produced far more that we could ever use ourselves. In fact, Dad was as generous as he could be with everyone and gave produce away by the bushel. When we had company from town he'd always say, "Here, y'all take some groceries home with you." He'd go to one of several freezers and fill a grocery bag with frozen veggies. If anyone said "No thanks" he would insist and keep on filling up their take-home bag. I miss that.

Early every spring we prepared the soil to plant. This meant going over the fallow ground with a tiller and working the edges with a hoe. There might be a few things left over from the fall garden, but most of it was unused during the winter. We'd get it turned over good and the weeds out of the way. Then he'd plant the seeds and I would help.

We always had field peas, butterbeans, several kinds of squash, okra, pole beans (Stacey calls them string beans), strawberries, asparagus, broccoli, cabbage, leaf lettuce, eggplant, several kinds of pepper including bell and banana, cantaloupe, carrots, radishes, onions, red potatoes, and at least one row of corn. We planted at least twelve different varieties of tomatoes, from cherry to beefsteak.

As the seeds grew and the tiny plants sprouted on the rows, it was my job to keep the weeds under control and to sprinkle Sevin dust to prevent bugs from attacking the small plants. I was also supposed to keep everything watered if it didn't rain. We did this with soaker hoses and sprinklers which had to be moved so that everything had adequate moisture. Fighting the weeds and bugs continued all summer, though we typically got plenty of rain.

The next big challenge was when things started producing in May and June. Harvesting butterbeans meant I sat on a bucket to save my back and dragged it forward along the row. I loved finding the strawberries but dreaded cutting the okra. I had to wear long sleeves and gloves because it was so itchy. If you didn't stay on top of it you'd end up with a lot of inedible okra because it became too hard and tough. The same was true for squash. If Dad found too much wasted okra or squash, he'd say, "Boy, I thought I told you to stay on top of that stuff. If you don't, you're going to have a problem with the end of my belt." He meant it, too. I was motivated to keep everything picked in a timely manner.

As we harvested the vegetables the process began for putting them up. Peas and butterbeans had to be shelled by hand and put in freezer bags. Pole beans were "snapped" and the strings pulled off before being cut up and stored the same way. The okra and squash were cut up and frozen as well. We pulled and shucked the corn, pulled off the silk, cut if off the cobb, and then Mom blanched it and froze it, too.

Some things had to be pickled and Mom put up figs and peaches that way. We ate most of the plums as we picked 'em. We consumed as much food as possible and gave away lots more. I was grown before I ever ate a slice of pizza or spaghetti, or an enchilada. My whole diet consisted almost entirely of home-grown vegetables, meat we raised, and cornbread.

When we lost the place to bankruptcy and moved to a rental house in town, one of the first things Dad did was plow up half the back yard and plant a garden. When he bought the new ranch in Hope Hull a year later, he planted a five-acre garden!

One year he planted a whole acre of corn for human consumption. By then, however, I was grown and mostly gone, so it fell on Linwood to carry on the gardening tradition with our Dad. I wasn't jealous. It's interesting to me that neither of us keep a garden today, but both Linwood and I live in the country and have plenty of room for one.

One of the most well-known passages in the Bible says that whatever a man sows, that shall he also reap. (Galatians 6:7, NLT) I learned the truth of it as a very young child when we planted in the springtime. If you wanted corn, you planted corn. When the harvest of corn happened, you couldn't change it by wishing. No, if you wanted a different harvest you had to plant a different seed. It's better to connect choice and consequence in advance. Then plant wisely. What are you planting?

I learned to work in that old garden, and I learned that work is necessary to produce the results we want in our lives. I also learned that there is a season for everything, and if we don't try to rush things, they typically work out in time. Sometimes we plant, sometimes we water and weed, and sometimes we reap the harvest. Timing is important, and God's grace helps us get it right. I also learned from my Dad's example that it's good thing to be generous when you have the opportunity to give something away, particularly if it's good to eat!

~~~~~~~~~~~~~~~~~~~~~~~~
~~~~~~~~~~~~~~~~~~~~~~~~

"I WATCHED"

I watched the sad frown that wouldn't go,
As the life he loved was loaded up and hauled away.
He leaned against the fence that grandaddy and he built,
And then he saw I frowned, too.

My childhood pastures gone like the wind,
Hard-earned ground, lush and green,
Honeysuckle hedgerows and buzzing bees,
And every blade a friend.

The bank said no when he wanted a yes,
The cattle sold months early and all was lost,
Barns and land and house and all,
And then we moved to town.

But he'd never stay, no sir,
Somehow in one short year found a way,
To move back to the country and breathe again,
A better place and way and time,

With cows and horses and grass-filled space,
Mama called it heaven's gate,
Because it felt like just that,
And the blessing they wished for.

I watched his sad frown that wouldn't go,
But it did, replaced by his soul's smile,
He leaned against the fence that he and I built,
And then he saw I smiled, too.
Yessir, I smiled, too.

~~~~~~~~~~~~~~~~~~~~~~~~~
~~~~~~~~~~~~~~~~~~~~~~~~~

Artist - Robert "Shoofly" Shufelt

"I once thought these things were valuable, but now I consider them worthless because of what Christ has done..."
Philippians 3:7 (NLT)

Paul wrote about gain and loss, value and appraisal. Someone has said, "Never trust a man who is unacquainted with loss. " Why? Someone who's never lost anything is challenged to appreciate the value of keeping it. Paul had an impressive set of credentials and accomplishments, including obeying God's law without fault. Yet in view of what Christ did to procure his salvation, Paul counted it all as worthless. When we are blessed, whether materially, relationally, or spiritually, it's good to appreciate the blessing. But all that we have is discounted when compared to the incomparable value of the atoning work of Jesus on the cross and what the gift of salvation does for us. It is in the light of the ultimate gift that all other gifts are accurately appraised.

Prayer Starter: Lord, help me to realize there is nothing more valuable than knowing You,

in Jesus' name.

"UNPLOWED GROUND"

I'm looking at my pasture,
Hoping for some winter wheat,
Need it for the grazing,
A good stand would be sweet.

But before we plant that seed,
We've got to break the ground,
Get that old soil ready,
'Fore the plantin' comes around.

And, yes, the ground is rocky,
And it has been so dry,
Takes some time to do it,
But we give it our best try.

'Cause if you don't make ready,
The seed, it cannot grow,
The harvest never happens,
If the soil's too hard to sow.

Get it plowed and ready,
Then get the seed all sown,
Pray the Good Lord sends some rain,
And bless the seed we've thrown.

God is the master sower,
The seed, His word that's true,
But if our hearts have not been plowed,
It's the next thing we should do.

Break up all that's hardened,
Let the Spirit have His way,
Receive the word that's planted,
And in everything obey.

And when the season's turning,
And the harvest time is near,
So glad you did the plowing,
When the fruit you want is here.

Lord, break up the fallow ground,
It's time Your face to seek,
Shower on us righteousness,
Lift up the tired and weak.

We'll praise You for the harvest,
For producing Kingdom fruit,
Your word is why it happened,
And in our hearts took root.

~~~~~~~~~~~~~~~~~~~~~~~~~
~~~~~~~~~~~~~~~~~~~~~~~~~

.".. break up your unplowed ground; for it is time to seek the Lord, until He comes and showers righteousness on you."
Hosea 10:12 (NIV)

Brokenness is something the great revivalists of church history often talked about. It was plowing up the hardened heart that prepared for the word and the moving of God's Spirit. When people humbled themselves and allowed their own egos to die, God was able to come in with His agenda and change people and situations eternally. It was God's work, no doubt about it. And God's Spirit cannot be manipulated. You cannot "make" revival happen. But great spiritual awakening is possible if we ask God to help us break up the unplowed ground of our hearts.

Lord, plow my heart and plant in me seeds of righteousness

____

____

____

____

____

____

____

____

____,

in Jesus' name.

COVEY RISE

My Dad was a bird hunter, and where we're from, that means he hunted quail. The best bird dog we ever had was named Bo, and he was as steady as any pointer could be. Dad and Bo were the dynamic duo of quail hunters. We hunted horseback, and Dad's 1000-acre dream ranch had a least fifty coveys of wild birds. We'd never heard of pen-raised quail back then.

When I was a kid, I rode with the men to hold their horses so when we found a covey, they could step off to shoot. They would hand me the reins, and I'd watch while they walked up the birds. I had to take a firm grip, because occasionally a horse might spook a little when the shotguns blasted. Bo never moved a muscle until the birds flew, and then Dad would say, "Dead, dead bird, Bo." And Bo would retrieve the downed quail and bring 'em to Dad. It was exciting for me to watch. Then, we'd ride on to the next covey.

When I was twelve years old Dad gave me my first shotgun for Christmas, a single-shot twenty gage. I was very proud of it! Time passed, and I no longer was expected to just hold the horses. I got to shoot! Dad taught me, and I practiced, but he was always the best shot I ever saw. Which brings me to the most unforgettable, perfect bird-hunting moment. It was magical.

My Uncle Ward was Dad's oldest brother. Uncle Ward and other relatives often came for Thanksgiving, all the way from South Carolina to Alabama. We always went hunting, and there was an ongoing argument between Dad and Ward about who was the best shot.

On this particular day, Dad, Uncle Ward, and I were the only hunters. We had found birds all day, and as the shadows lengthened and the sun dropped lower, we turned our horses toward home. Within sight of the horse trailer, Bo pointed. It was an open pasture with little cover, just a few scrubby bushes along a fence line, and not where you would typically find quail.

I remember the sun was setting and the sky was on fire with gold and pink beauty. There was a cool breeze blowing toward us, and I had turned the collar of my hunting jacket up. Bo pointed like he always did, but Dad doubted him. "Maybe old Bo is tired and these are just grass birds, but we'd better go see. Hold the horses, Brad."

As the two men dismounted, pulled their shotguns, and handed me the reins, I heard Dad say, "Ward, why don't we decide this once and for all about who's the best shot?"

In his gravelly, gruff voice, Ward said, "Why don't you just hush and hunt, Paul Bradley."

They walked the few steps to where Bo held his point, Ward on the left and Dad on the right, and then it happened. I bet you fifty birds rose, fanning out in front of them, and both men shot twice. Boom-boom! In that split-second, each had downed two birds. And then a quail got up at Dad's feet and flew in the opposite direction but to the right. Dad whirled and then boom, the bird fell. Three birds on a covey rise! "Dead, dead bird, Bo." I knew I had seen something I'd never forget.

As we loaded the horses and Dad cranked the truck, Uncle Ward was silent. Dad said, "Well, I guess that settled it, then." He grinned.

Uncle Ward gruffly mumbled, "Hush and drive, Paul Bradley." And that was that .

Bo died a long time ago. I still sometimes miss that dog. Dad left for heaven in 2001. I miss him. Time has a funny way of catching up with me but I will never forget that perfect fall day. My words can't do it justice. Psalm 118:24 (ESV) comes to mind again. *"This is the day the Lord has made; let us rejoice and be glad in it."* I know it sounds like a simple time, but to me it was perfect. A boy hunting with his Dad and uncle, a-horseback together. A perfect dog. A perfect shot. It just doesn't get much better.

~~~~~~~~~~~~~~~~~~~~~~~~~~
~~~~~~~~~~~~~~~~~~~~~~~~~~

"HORSE NAMED HALLELUJAH"

We knew the mare was dying,
As she struggled to give birth,
And God knows that I loved her,
More than most things on this earth.

Lived long enough to give him,
The first milk that he'd need,
She then stopped drinkin' water,
And went off all her feed.

And though we tried to save her,
Nothing the vet could do,
We had my Grandma prayin',
For a miracle, it's true.

But then she wasn't breathing,
Her strong, old heartbeat failed,
And I ran home to Grandma,
And cried and fussed and wailed.

But then we prayed together,
And I heard her giving praise,
For the the time the mare once gave us,
All those happy, golden days.

Then she ended with an amen,
And a hallelujah, see,
So I decided then and there,
That's what his name would be.

The horse named Hallelujah,
Grew up and very strong,
Faster than all others,
And I never thought it wrong,

To match him up and race him,
'Cause he never got outrun,
Though he would surprise them,
I thought it so much fun.

And, Dad, he said let's cut him,
He'll make a cow horse, see,
I said, no, let's race him,
He's breeding stock to be.

But not like some stud horses,
With ease to work and train,
And I believe the reason,
Is he had his momma's brain.

And every time we won a race,
The noise was loud and clear,
They shouted hallelujah,
You heard it far and near.

It's been many decades,
Since that grand, old studhorse died,
And he was a great pleasure,
To know and breed and ride.

And as we laid him gently low,
The night he said good-bye,
I whispered hallelujah,
With a teardrop in my eye.

And friends who stood there with me,
Said they heard it on the wind,
A hallelujah chorus,
Praises for the life that ends.

That's what I hope will happen,
When they finally lay me low,
At the moment of my passing,
I hope that what we show,

Is a praise to our Creator,
And to Jesus Christ, our friend,
Who's there with Hallelujah,
Where God's pastures never end.

"Surely Your goodness and unfailing love will pursue me all the days of my life, and I will live in the house of the Lord forever..."
Psalm 23:6 (NLT)

Living forever with the Lord is the best thing about the twenty-third Psalm. Yes, everything about it is wonderful- rest in great pastures, renewal of strength, guidance and protection, overflowing blessings- all of it! But, best of all is not what we experience here in this life. The Lord shepherds us here so that He can live forever with us there. All of this life is not about here but there. And it's important to remember how we can be sure we are going there. Assurance comes when we trust Jesus to do something for us that we cannot do for ourselves. When we surrender control to Him, He exchanges control for assurance. If He makes us sure, we will never be talked out of it by anything as paltry as a mere argument. That's because we've experienced His goodness and mercy.

Prayer starter: Lord, give me the full assurance that when I die I will live with You forever,

____

____

____

____

____

____

___________________________,

in Jesus' name.

RENDERING TRUCK

Back in Alabama, a town person once asked me how many cattle were in our herd. This person didn't know that the question itself was bad manners. That's just not something I ever thought was okay to ask anyone. Call me old school, or just plain old, I guess. The person who asked the question envisioned a perfect pastoral scene with a herd of mother cows, baby calves by their sides, and maybe a few bulls standing nearby. But that's not the kind of cattle business we had.

Dad was a trader and an order buyer, we didn't own a year to year, tenured herd of registered or commercial livestock with a breeding program. It's not that we never had mother cows, 'cause sometimes Dad would buy a whole herd of them, keep 'em till they birthed calves, and typically sell 'em all as "pairs". We were definitely in the cattle business. And at the peak of it, we had as many as a dozen trucks running the roads twenty-four seven.

We always had orders to fill. People from all over the country would call Dad looking for cattle. They'd talk about the cattle market and tell Dad what they were trying to buy. Most would usually want replacement heifers or killer cows or yearlings, or whatever. Dad would strike a deal to buy them for a certain amount, then added delivery costs and his commission. He brokered the cattle, which meant we handled a lot of them as they came in by truck from the auctions where they were purchased. When we had enough to ship out an order, they were loaded up and sent.

Many of our trucks went west to Texas, Oklahoma, and Kansas. He also did deals in the country, buying cattle straight from the producers and shipping them to those who had made an order. We handled a lot of Florida cattle in those days, and some from the gulf coast of Mississippi. There was always cowboy work involved when livestock like that had to be gathered.

In addition to the bull haulers coming and going, every fall Dad would buy bull yearlings. We usually ran about a thousand head annually. We'd receive 'em, castrate, brand, worm, implant, ear tag and doctor 'em. Then they would be turned out on native pasture to graze for a year. All of 'em were sold in late summer or early fall of the next year, and then the whole process started over. There was a lot of cowboy work looking after them, too.

When you fool with a lot of cattle, many of them are sick and have to be doctored. Cattle. I never saw anybody better at doctoring and helping sick cattle get well than my Dad. In my eyes, he worked wonders with 'em! Inevitably, some of them didn't make it. Finding dead cattle in the pens and the lots was a fact of life and an ever-present reality. I learned about death as a kid, and there was very little emotion involved.

Once a week, the rendering truck paid us a visit. It was actually a dump truck that this company had customized and would send around to pick up dead cattle. As you might imagine, driving a rendering truck was a nasty job, it was smelly and messy and nothing pleasant about it. It certainly was a valuable service to an operation like ours. In the past, renderers paid for dead animals. I believe the carcasses were processed to make pet food and fertilizer. When the rendering truck came around, Dad would put a chain on the dead animal and drag it out into the lane in front of our working barn with a tractor. Sometimes there would be only one, and sometimes more.

One Friday afternoon the rendering truck came and we had one for him to take away. It was one of those chronics that didn't make it. She was a little old, thin Hereford heifer. Dad had bought her cheap at the sale in Robertsdale, and we did our best to get her well, but she was just too far gone. She laid in the lane with a chain around her and I watched as the truck backed up to load her.

Dad happened to be nearby, and when the driver pulled up, Dad noticed that there was an animal on the rendering truck that was still alive. Horrible, right? It was another Hereford heifer piled in with the dead ones. I'm sure she was sick and someone must have thought she wouldn't make it but when she kicked a time or two, Dad saw an opportunity.

Dad ran up to the driver and told him He'd trade the dead one for the live one. The fellow was shocked. He'd probably never heard an offer like that before. In fact that's exactly what he said, shaking his head. Then he grinned, "Well, Mr. Paul, I'm not supposed to do anything like dat, but I guess it'll be all right dis time." I watched while the fellow climbed up in the truck, lowered the back of it down, and dragged the heifer off. We then helped him get the dead one loaded. Dad shook hands with him and off he went.

The newly rescued heifer was lying flat and couldn't get up at first. After a bunch of pushing and pulling, we got her sitting in an upright position. Dad sent me to the barn office to get medicine and a syringe. He shot her in the neck with antibiotics. He then sent me to get a five gallon bucket for water and hay for her. The water was almost too heavy for me to carry but I got it done. I struggled with it, sloshing some of it out on my boots. I climbed up in the nearby hay loft of the barn and threw down a bale of good coastal hay for her. Dad took out his old Case pocketknife and cut the strings. We broke it up and put the hay where she could reach it. We also gave her a little sweet feed.

It was early spring if I remember right, with warm days and cool nights, but he thought she'd be okay since she wasn't far from the barn which would serve as a wind break. The next morning I jumped out of the bed to check on her. I really expected to find the heifer dead, but she wasn't. In fact, she was up and grazing on a little patch of grass over to the side of the barn lane. When I saw her, I was glad that I remembered to close all the gates, or she might have escaped! Her nose and eyes were still runny and she had a cough, but she was up and eating. We gave her another shot and turned her out into the hospital pasture nearby.

A few months went by. Dad watched her carefully. We doctored her. We fed her. We cared for her. She put on weight, got stronger, her nose cleared up and her cough disappeared. The end of the story is that this heifer survived and was later sold for a profit. It was a rendering truck success story that I never forgot. If my Dad hadn't of been present or been quick to make the trade, that heifer would have died under a heap of carcasses. Jesus does that for us, he watches us, offers nourishment for our souls, pulls us out of the grave and restores us. Turns out that trading death for life is something God wants us all to know and experience for ourselves.

"But God will redeem my soul from the power of the grave, for He shall receive me."
Psalm 49:15 (NKJV)

"Very truly I tell you, a time is coming and has now come when the dead will hear the voice of the Son of God and those who hear will live."
John 5:25 (NIV)

"I will ransom them from the power of the grave; I will redeem them from death...."
Hosea 13:14 (NKJV)

"WAYWARD SOUL"

The wayward soul to be made whole,
Must come to God above.
The Shepherd seeks, that sheep who reeks,
But needs to know His love.

He goes in search outside the church,
To find the one that's lost.
He ranges far, sets high the bar,
But glad to pay the cost.

The cowboys true, the ones I knew,
Who horseback sought to find,
The bovine wild, and rode and smiled,
When casting out their twine,

To bring one back, take up the slack,
And save those that escape,
Kept on till they, had found that stray,
Though some were in bad shape.

I see there, the Shepherd's care,
For those who wayward go,
Love so fine, and yes, divine,
To bring them home and so,

What Jesus said, it's why He bled,
To bring us home for good,
Sheep, coin and son, and for just one,
He did all that He could.

What will we do, it's nothing new,
When rescue is God's plan,
Sit and wait, beside the gate,
Or go and find that man.

To seek and save, His life He gave,
And we should give ours, too,
Because He came and called our name,
It's the least that we can do.

~~~~~~~~~~~~~~~~~~~~
~~~~~~~~~~~~~~~~~~~~

"Won't He leave the ninety-nine others in the wilderness and go to search for the one that is lost until he finds it?"
Luke 15:4 (NLT)

In response to the criticism that Jesus associated with "notorious sinners," He told a set of three stories. The first about a lost sheep, the second, a lost coin, and the third, a lost son. The point of all three is that people who need help are worth going after. Jesus wanted everyone to know that this was the heavenly Father's heart, to seek and save the lost. There are many problems that arise when we take this view of God seriously. It gives us personal hope and that's a good thing. But it also challenges us to care in ways that are inconvenient, expensive, and unselfish. Are we willing for the God who seeks sinners to seek them through us?

Prayer Starter: Lord, use me to go after the wayward soul,

____

____

____

____

____

____

____

in Jesus' name.

BACK TO TEXAS

It was cold that winter in Alabama and I was fed up. I spent most of my time taking care of my Dad's eight hundred-plus yearlings, and a smaller percentage trying to sell real estate with his firm. Problem was, the interest rate was over twenty per cent, and we didn't have a new loan on any real estate transaction in over a year! Plus, Dad and I didn't get along too well. But that's another story...

Anyway, I decided I needed to go, and back to Texas sounded good to me. I had an old friend in Weatherford who wanted to hire me to sell livestock mineral supplements. I also applied for a job with Nocona Boot Company and had an interview lined up with them. So the adventure was on.

I drove an old car my mother had given me after I turned mine over and totaled it coming home drunk after a rodeo. This car was what you'd call a "land yacht." It was a big, long, heavy 1969 Plymouth Fury with over 200,000 miles on it. It was white with a gold interior. I had 'em install a hitch so I could pull my stock trailer behind it. It was an old, open trailer, painted dark blue, but it had a good floor and all but one of the lights worked. By "open" I mean it had no roof.

After getting everything ready to go, I realized I needed more room for my stuff- tack, saddles and pads, ropes, shotgun, clothes, etc. So I removed the back seat and left it in my folks' storage room. (Later Mom had to send it to me so I could sell the car.). Basically everything I owned was in that car, either in the trunk or what used to be the back seat. And, of course, with my good, gray gelding, Drifter, in the trailer.

I had bought Drifter from an ad in the Ft. Worth Star-Telegram. It read: Registered Gray Gelding For Sale, $800, and the phone number. I met the owner, rode the horse and immediately liked him. She met me a couple days later at the Cow Belle Arena in Mansfield, Texas so I could see if you could rope off this horse. She thought so, but wasn't sure. It was a practice night, and when I backed him into the roping box he did fine. When I nodded for the steer, he tracked him perfectly and turned off just right when I roped the steer. I bought him, and took him home to Alabama when I later moved. Now we were going back to Texas, his face in the cold wind.

We did fine till we crossed the Mississippi River into Louisiana. I heard a crash, and looked back to see the tail gate of the trailer somersaulting down the side of the highway! I guess all the baling wire had come loose, and thank God no other vehicles were near. I pulled over, and walked back to where it lay, then carried and dragged the dern thing up the side of the road. I got it re-installed.

I guess Drifter was too cold to care. He never blinked, that I could tell. Once I got everything tied on, wired on, and checked on, we hit the road again. It took us about thirteen hours to get to Ft. Worth. My cowboy buddy, Jerry, let me keep Drifter at his place, and another old friend, Charlie, let me use his spare bedroom in Burleson till I could get my own place. I was set.

I had the Nocona interview and got to meet Larry Mahan, but they wanted me to move to Vernon, Texas, and I was too broke to do it. So, I took the job selling cow feed. I was excited, but looking back I realize how little I actually had at that time. It just goes to show that some of life's best times and im-portant moments don't depend on money, wealth, or material possessions. The best things never do...

~~~~~~~~~~~~~~~~~~~~~~~~~

"Keep your lives free from the love of money and be content with what you have, because God has said, "Never will I leave you; never will I forsake you."
Hebrews 13:5 (NIV)
~~~~~~~~~~~~~~~~~~~~~~~~~

"ZIPPO"

Way back in my younger days,
I loved to start those colts always,
And one big gray he was unfazed,
By all I put him through.

'Bout third ride he did not buck,
I thought it was all good luck,
But all about to come unstuck,
The truth I'm telling you.

I reached into my pocket then,
I used to smoke those lights back when,
Fired up my zippo, yes, a sin,
My pony broke in half.

My confidence was overplayed,
And quickly the mistake I made,
I wish now I had delayed,
That smoke, I had to laugh.

Meanwhile I held both the reins,
Taking all the greatest pains,
To get his head up, use my brains,
To stop this bucking fit.

But suddenly the right rein broke,
That pony never missed a stroke,
And headed to the fence, no joke,
No sign that he would quit.

Just before he hit the wire,
I stepped off, he did not tire,
But stopped as if he lost desire,
And acted like he's broke.

That was when I realized,
My pinky he had traumatized,
Broke the knuckle, no surprise,
Because I lit that smoke.

Led that horse around and round,
Quickly he was all calmed down,
Stepped back on no problem found,
In spite of pinkie pain.

Later on I clearly thought,
Maybe learn the lesson taught,
Been better if I hadn't brought,
My pride aboard that train.

Sometimes that finger in the night,
Lets me know it's not all right,
Grew back crooked, what a sight,
Not something you forget.

Reminds me of what pride can do,
Injury and no doubt true,
God resists in me and you,
With no exceptions yet.

~~~~~~~~~~~~~~~~~~~~~~~~~~~

"All of you, clothe yourselves with humility toward one another, because God opposes the proud but gives grace to the humble..."
1 Peter 5:5 (NIV)

There are no exceptions to this rule. God always opposes the proud and always gives grace to the humble. When our pride gets the best of us, God resists our egotism in order to teach us to walk humbly with Him. Humility is the grace-trigger for every need and every new step of faith. It's sometimes a hard and painful lesson, but it's always worth it because of the grace that floods the humble. Count on it.

Lord, help me to humble myself so that I may receive Your grace...

____

____
____
____
___________________in Jesus' name.
~~~~~~~~~~~~~~~~~~~~~~~~~~~

UNCLE ROY

I was mad at God...It sounds ridiculous, but it's honestly the way I felt. When I reached important intersections in my life, I had prayed for God's direction and received advice from Christian people I trusted. Still, I had managed to make unwise choices that brought miserable results. I blamed the Lord. And there was misery inside of me. I felt betrayed and as a result, had dropped out of church and pretty much told God to stay the hell out of my life. But He didn't...

I was running the roads in central Texas. I owned a little place in the country and day worked and team roped on week-ends. I drank too much, especially when things bothered me, and whenever I thought of my past relationship with the Lord, my heart winced. Then the letter...

One day I drove to pick up the mail at the downtown post office in Waco, and there, mixed in with the bills, was a letter from my Uncle Roy McClain. He was my Dad's brother and was a very prominent Baptist preacher. He has been pastor of First Baptist Church in Atlanta on old Peachtree Street for many years, preceding Charles Stanley. He retired for seven years, and then left retirement to pastor the First Baptist Church of

"

Orangeburg, South Carolina, his original pastorate as a young man. That was the letter's postmark.

I sat in my pick-up truck and looked at the envelope. My mind flashed back to times spent with Uncle Roy. He was always larger-than-life to me, and the river of energy that flowed from him spilled out on all of us and filled the room. He had red hair, piercing eyes, and a quick wit. An artist, musician, scholar, author, karateka, antique-collector, world traveler, WW II veteran, horseman- all were parts of his very diverse experience and personality. And, he could really preach. We hadn't talked in well over a year, and I wondered why on earth he had written a letter to me now.

I took off my cowboy hat and laid it on the seat beside me, then opened the letter with my pocketknife. The words were typed, single-spaced on the church letterhead, and the message was clear. He said: "You've zigged and zagged a lot in your young life, but God has made an investment in you, and He's calling to account now. Life is too short to grind it away in real or imagined guilt and grief. And all men used by God have walked the razor edge of faith and fear, belief and cynicism."

He continued: "The great sin in life is not so much in falling down, but in the stupidity of not getting back up. Or, in staying down so long you swear down is up. And the woods are full of those kind of fools, inside the church and out. So, get up!" And then he invited me to come see him in South Carolina.

I sat in the truck for awhile trying to process his words. I shed tears, almost to the point of embarrassing myself and, for a minute, pretty much lost control of my feelings. Those two words, "get up," kept repeatedly swirling around in my mind, and I could hear them in Uncle Roy's resonant voice. The bitterness inside of me broke, and I turned TO, not away from the grace.

There is no doubt in my mind that Uncle Roy's letter was one of those unforgettable moments when God makes sure you know He's not finished with you.

The long and short of it is, I got up.

Maybe you're reading this, and you feel distant from God. Betrayed. Maybe even unworthy. Maybe you feel like you're too far gone. The Bible tells us we're never too far gone and nothing is able to separate us from the Lord's love. Romans 8:38-39 assures us in these words: *"For I am convinced that neither death nor life, neither angels nor demons, neither the present nor the future, nor any powers, neither height nor depth, nor anything else in all creation, will be able to separate us from the love of God that is in Christ Jesus our Lord."*

~~~~~~~~~~~~~~~~~~~~~~~~~
~~~~~~~~~~~~~~~~~~~~~~~~~

"FIND A WAY"

Find a way or make one,
They said it long ago,
And many in my circle,
Say cowboy up, let's go!

And I admire that sentiment,
To make that old wheel turn,
Get out there and get 'er done,
Don't let that daylight burn.

My people knew they had to work,
Not up to someone else,
If it is to be it's up to me,
Let tighten up our belts.

And I've found a way or made one,
For many years of try,
But here's something that I have learned,
And it's the truth, no lie.

And that's sometimes you gotta wait,
For God to make a way,
And if you run ahead of Him,
You always have to pay,

More that what you want to,
When what I should have done,
Was let God open up the door,
Before I made my run.

Waiting isn't lazy,
Or some entitlement,
But seeing if God's timing,
Is really being sent.

And when you really know it's time,
To ready, aim and shoot,
You'll find you hit the target,
And have more peace to boot.

So find a way or make one,
But put it in God's hands,
Wait on His direction,
'Cause you can trust His plans.

~~~~~~~~~~~~~~~~~~~~~~~~~~
~~~~~~~~~~~~~~~~~~~~~~~~~~

"Wait for the Lord; be strong and take heart and wait for the Lord."
Psalm 27:14 (NIV)

I've always had the feeling that God was waiting on me. My attitude was do something, and if it was wrong, God would correct me. But sometimes waiting on the Lord means just that, waiting, and it is necessary if we want to hear and ultimately do God's will. I'm not naturally very patient. But this is a part of the Spirit's fruit, and though it may not be easy, it is crucial that we get it right. God knows what he wants us to do and when He wants us to do it. Being ready means we trust both His will and his timing.

Prayer Starter: Lord, teach me to wait on You...

____

____

____

____

____

____

____

____

, in Jesus' name.

SELL YOUR SADDLE

Sometimes life just twists and turns in unexpected ways. I don't pretend to know why everything happens the way it does, but I've learned that the Lord is always with us, no matter the mess we get ourselves into. He was with me through a very bad season of my life when I was angry with Him and blamed Him for my misfortune. Through it all, He was always faithful, in spite of my bitterness.

I made some mistakes in my life and after bouncing around awhile, I took a job with an old friend selling livestock supplements in Texas. I was living in Ft. Worth and went calling on customers all over central Texas. I loved the work, the cowboy culture and the people.

My 2nd wife and I moved to Waco and I began to sell feed in a seven county area. Mostly I focused on the many thousands of yearlings that were turned out on wheat or oats all over that country. As many as a hundred thousand head were pastured in Falls County alone. I only knew one person in Waco when we moved there, a fellow named Tom Felton. But Tom introduced me around and I developed a network of customers.

I team roped and drank whiskey on weekends. During the week, I sold and delivered feed and day worked for my new ranching friends. We were able to buy a few acres in Hallsburg and life was good, at least it was better than it had been. Of course I never went to church because I still had a bad attitude toward the Lord.

One Sunday morning I woke up with a bad hangover. I loaded up on coffee and Advil and began surfing channels on television. It was too early for the football games and I wasn't interested in watching a news program, so I kept flipping the channel till I ran across a preacher who captured my attention. He brought a strong message and was a dynamic speaker. He reminded me of the revival preachers I had heard while growing up as a kid in church. At the end of the program they said his name was Rev. Dick Freeman, pastor of First United Methodist Church in downtown Waco. I couldn't believe he was local or that he was Methodist. I decided to go hear him.

The week flew past and when Sunday rolled around again, we loaded up and went to hear Dick Freeman. He made you feel like he was speaking directly to you and was even better in person than on television. We went back several Sundays. I was working really hard during the week and was still playing hard on weekends, but on Sunday morning I decided that's where we needed to be.

After several weeks I decided I would make an appointment with Freeman and go talk with him. As a teenager I had a real conversion experience and for ten years actively served the Lord. I had been involved in youth ministry and during that time had received a call to preach. A lot of life happened after that initial calling and I had begun to believe it was too late to think about ministry or preaching.

The day came to go talk with the pastor, and I walked in wearing my everyday boots and hat. In those days I wore my hair on the longish side and sported a big furry beard. I always carried a can of Skoal in my pocket so combine the boots and hair and tobacco can, I imagine I looked like I just came in off the range. Rev. Freeman's secretary wasn't too sure about me, but Pastor Freeman was warm as he greeted me at the door of his office.

Freeman was a nice man, inviting and very relatable. His wife's family owned a big ranch in south Texas so he was familiar with the cattle business. He began asking me questions about my life and was very attentive as I told him my story. He was particularly interested in how I came to know the Lord and the ways I had served in the past.

He didn't offer much advice, just said how glad he was that we were attending and hoped we would join the church. I remember that he was very encouraging, and prayed a prayer with me before I left. I felt very positive about our time together.

Several weeks later we joined the church and were warmly welcomed by everyone. Shortly after we joined and I began to be more involved with a body of believers, I felt a very strong pull toward getting my life right with the Lord. Dick Freeman's messages every Sunday were a big part of what was happening to me. His words spoke to me, made me think. Finally one week day I decided to make things right.

One morning after my wife went on to work, I lay down in the middle of the living room floor, determined not to get up until I knew I had gotten right with God. I felt like the light had left because so much had happened in my life, so many mistakes, so may wrong turns. I didn't know how to talk to God and I didn't really know where to start. So I just started confessing every bad thing I had done until I was cried out and confessed out. As I cried and as I confessed, I felt like the Lord was right there, not holding me at arm's length but inviting me to go on with Him right then. I kept hearing "Let's go!" over and over in my mind. I knew it was the Lord speaking to me.

I began to live differently. I began to think differently. I met with Dick several several times and he knew how I was feeling. Any time, however, that I mentioned the ministry he said, "We don't really need any more good old boys in the Methodist ministry" and I would always respond with, "That's exactly what I hoped you would say." But after several more months, I continued to feel the Lord calling me into ministry so I went back to see Freeman.

"I know what you said about the ministry not needing any more good old boys, Dick, but this feeling just won't go away. What should I do?"

He said, "I knew if your feelings didn't go away it was the Lord calling you so that is exactly what you should do. Go into the ministry."

I had graduated from college ten years before, but he encouraged me to apply to seminary and be prepared to move. So, without hesitation, I applied to seminary and began to downsize my life. In order to go to seminary, I needed to sell pretty much everything we had. Over time I sold my three horses, our home and acreage, my truck, and my business.

As the time grew closer for us to move, I realized that we needed to downsize even more. I had a large tack room full of cowboy gear and my neighbor, who was a Christian and a cowboy, came by and bought whatever he thought he needed. I parted with bridles, saddle pads, halters, hobbles, chaps, and an assortment of other odds and ends. He asked, "What would you take for that saddle?" I paused at his question. I owned a very nice roping saddle that I had ridden for a decade or more, and it had never crossed my mind to sell it. I answered pretty quickly that it was not for sale.

That night I couldn't sleep. You see, there's this unwritten cowboy rule that says, "Never sell your saddle." My guess is that this one piece of cowboy gear is so directly tied to your identity that you would never want to let it go. I suppose that's why it never occurred to me that I should sell it. I asked the Lord about it. I literally prayed about my saddle.

"Isn't it enough that I sold my horses, this place and my truck?" I asked God. He didn't respond with an answer. No feeling. No answer. Nothing. I finally went on to sleep, but was still struggling with it when I woke up next morning. I called my neighbor and quoted him a price on the saddle. He came by after work that day with a check, and just like that, my old cack was gone. But I had peace.

Some may not understand the struggle. It wasn't that my saddle was evil or good, but it was a symbol of my identity as a man. The Lord was redefining all that inside of me during that season of my life. I sold my saddle because I did not want to hold back a single thing from Him. I sold everything except for the necessities. With nothing more than faith and a shoe string, we moved and I started graduate school.

The lesson I had to learn is that until you die to yourself, you cannot truly live. Until you surrender your plan, it will compete with God's best. Decades have passed since I sold that saddle, since I attended seminary and received my graduate degree, since I gave it all to God. . I've spent many years in Christian ministry and now, all these years later, I have some acres in Texas, have a string of good horses and a start up herd of longhorn cattle. I even have a room full of bridles, saddle pads, halters, hobbles, chaps, and an assortment of other odds and ends. And I don't just have one saddle, I have several.

Though I am thankful for the leather and conchos that now line my tack room, I am more thankful that God always had a plan for me. I am thankful he brought me from darkness into light. I simply had to let go of the small stuff and follow Him.

~~~~~~
~~~~~~

"Then Jesus told His disciples, "If anyone would come after me, let him deny himself and take up his cross and follow me." **Matthew 16:24 (ESV)**

"My sheep hear my voice, and I know them, and they follow me." **John 10:27 (ESV)**

"Again Jesus spoke to them saying, "I am the light of the world. Whoever follows me will not walk in darkness, but will have the light of life." **John 8:12 (ESV)**

".........He found Phillip and said, "Follow Me". **John 1:43 (ESV)**

"HE RODE "

When his daddy set him on that horse,
He laughed and clapped his hands,
Just a happy three-year-old,
On those distant pasture lands.

And he rode and rode and rode...

When he was twelve they gave to him,
A pretty zebra dun,
Came plumb from Oklahoma,
And man that horse could run.

When it came time to gather steers,
Or catch the wild bovine,
He'd trot out with the cowboy crew,
And never missed a time.

And he rode and rode and rode...

Dad got old and finally died,
The pasture lands were sold,
He found a way to stay horseback,
Though hard to take ahold.

Raised his children, grandkids, too,
Folks died whom he loved,
He'd catch a horse and saddle up,
When push came hard and shoved.

And he rode and rode and rode...

One day hooked his trailer up,
Got his horses loaded then,
Off to Texas with his love,
He'd not look back again.

And now an older, weathered man,
But not too old to ride,
He'll throw a leg and still step on,
And in you I'll confide,

From Bama out to Texas,
As far as Idaho,
Great Basin ranges way up there,
And he was glad to go.

And he rode and rode and rode...

Sometimes out there a-horseback,
He'll hear God's whisper say,
Time will come you'll ride with Me,
He looks forward to that day.

When the Lord will call him home,
No one knows just when,
With Jesus on a great white horse,
Forevermore and then,

He'll ride and ride and ride.

~~~~~~~~~~~~~~~~~~~~~~~~~

"Because of our faith, Christ has brought us into this place of undeserved privilege where we now stand, and we confidently and joyfully look forward to sharing God's glory."
Romans 5:2 (NLT)

Life has its blessings and challenges. There are seasons of enjoyment and seasons of trial and trouble. In it all and through it all God is with us. He loves us and knows what we need to be at peace and content. He is the giver of every good and perfect gift. But, in the end, life is not about this world. It is all about eternity. Our salvation is a gift that we cannot earn but must receive by faith. We can know and be fully assured that when the end of life comes we will immediately go to be with the Lord. He wants everyone to enjoy that assurance, but it comes only when we are willing to surrender ourselves to Him.
~~~~~~~~~~~~~~~~~~~~~~~~~

Prayer Starter: Lord, give me the full assurance of salvation, help me...

____

____

____

____

____

____

____

_________________________________ in Jesus' name.

ARMADILLO ROPING

Linwood was living in Mississippi while pursuing his banking career. It had been a while since I had seen him. He had been talking to a horse trader named Howard Fewell in Mendenhall and let him know he was seriously looking to purchase a good horse. I was excited when my brother called to let me know Howard found him one, a nice bay gelding.

Linwood had already found a good place to keep him so when he picked him up from Howard, he drove to his friend's several hundred-acre farm, backed him out of the trailer, and stepped on. He was smooth under the saddle. It was perfect, except I wish I could ride with him. I was between horses at that time and hadn't had a chance to ride in a while so when Linwood called and said the fellow who owned the farm had several saddle horses I could ride, I was ready.

We planned a Saturday ride in a couple of weeks and I could hardly wait. I got out my old roping saddle, wiped it down and oiled it up so I'd be ready. On the Friday night before our ride, I could hardly sleep. I set my alarm for 4:00 A.M. but woke up at 3:00 and made my coffee. I was in the truck and gone long before I needed to leave. In the predawn darkness I crossed Mobile Bay and through west Mobile out highway 98. South

Alabama was still asleep, and the traffic was light. The morning was perfect. I drove into the long, gravel driveway of the Mississippi farm two hours later, just as the pink started to show in the eastern sky.

Linwood arrived within minutes. He pulled a bucket of feed from his truck, and called in his new horse. He was a nice looking, well-built animal with a strong hip and pretty head. I was really happy for him but a tad envious. Some people will never understand how it feels when a person who is raised horseback has not ridden in a while, for whatever reason. It's like being thirsty on a hot day and anticipating a long, cold drink or being hungry and looking forward to a delicious meal. That's what I was feeling as Linwood saddled his mount and I looked at the other horses.

It didn't take me long to pick out a long-legged sorrel mare that seemed gentle. I normally would have chosen a gelding, but she was the best looking one in the lot. I got her saddled and spent a short while doing some groundwork. She moved off easily, stopped, and backed okay. The fellow who owned the place rode with us, but he was a very inexperienced rider. We were a little worried that he might have a mishap, but our beginning was good.

By the time the sun was coming up over the hardwoods and pines of this beautiful farm of rolling hills and grassy pastures, we could see the well-worn trails ahead of us. It was a beautiful, cool fall morning with a nice breeze blowing. It felt good. Just when everything felt perfect, suddenly, the sorrel mare balked in the trail. She just stopped and refused to follow Linwood's horse.

I shook my head a minute and I coaxed and clucked to her, then turned her in a tight circle. But still she refused to go forward so I tapped her with my spurs. That seemingly gentle mare reared straight up and fell over backwards! Fortunately, I was able to slide off her hindquarters without getting hurt. It was the first and only time I have ever ridden a horse that did that, and we could hardly believe she did it, as gentle as she acted.

The owner of the farm was scared to death at the event and apologized profusely. As any experienced cowboy would do, I led her around a bit, then stepped back on her and off we went. She acted like nothing had happened, but I stayed extra-alert the remainder of the ride. I laughed to think of that horse falling over. Proof that things can get western in Mississippi.

Up and down the hills we rode, and occasionally spooked a deer in the nearby brush. There were a variety of birds, including a big, red-tailed hawk that flew right over us. It was a fine day riding through God's creation. As we crossed a large pasture, we jumped an armadillo that scurried toward the trees at the other side of the field. We could see that he stopped on the edge. We stopped too. I smiled and took down my rope.

Linwood asked, "What are you going to do?".

"I thought I might rope me a Mississippi armadillo today," I whispered.

"You better watch that horse," he laughed. "You don't know what she'll do if you twirl a rope over her head."

"I was born careful," I assured him. He shook his head and laughed. The owner stood in silence. He may have even held his breath. We rode slowly and quietly across the pasture to get close to the armadillo that had squatted beside a cedar bush.

I built my loop as we rode and I twirled it a time or two and the sorrel mare didn't seem to care. When we got about twelve feet from the little armored target, I reined the mare to a stop, stood up in my stirrups, and sailed my rope toward the armadillo. I put it right over him. I tried to pull my slack in time to catch him, but it was impossible. He ran away into the woods as I coiled up my rope. It was quite an experience and to this day, it's the only time I tried to rope an armadillo.

On our way back to the barn we talked about growing up. Of horseback days. Of all the things we had experienced together, and the many cattle through the years we had moved, caught, and doctored. As we relived old memories, I remembered the words of Winston Churchill who wrote: "There is something about the outside of a horse that is good for the inside of a man." I agreed then. I agree now. It did my insides good to ride that day, even though the story would be better if I had caught that derned armadillo.

Looking back, it is another example that life moves too fast sometimes. The best moments are the ones we savor and later relive. Some people are so busy making a living they forget to live. We need to live life while we're able. If you're going through your days, forgetting to live, today is the day to start anew. Today is the day the Lord has made, let's live it.

~~~~~~~~~~~~~~~~~~~~~~~~~

"This is the day the Lord has made; we will rejoice and be glad in it." **Psalm 118:24 (NLT)**

~~~~~~~~~~~~~~~~~~~~~~~~~

"ROPING ARMADILLOS"

Got reset in the saddle,
And took a deeper breath,
I knew I had been rattled,
This scared me half to death.

How can an armadillo,
Cause this big a fuss,
For a horse this seasoned,
And so broke you can trust.

Maybe it was the sunlight,
Just 'fore the sun goes down,
A-shining through the tree limbs,
Right down to the ground.

Or maybe that thing snortin',
And running really fast,
Right at his feet so quickly,
Before he made his pass.

Old Strait he went to pitchin',
Like he never has before,
And I was pulling leather,
And tryin' to get some more.

I think I got it figured out,
I never should have tried,
To rope that little critter,
Just let him scoot on by.

Just thought it might be somethin',
A story I could tell,
Catch one good armadillo,
My how my pride would swell.

But you know that I missed him,
I threw right where he'd been,
Thank God I didn't catch him,
'Cause Strait was buckin' then.

Oh well, no real harm done,
I'm in my saddle seat,
Headed in by sundown,
And not down on my feet.

The Good Lord keeps us humble,
And I've had so much worse,
Than roping armadillos,
And so I'll end this verse.

~~~~~~~~~~~~~~~~~~~~~~~~
~~~~~~~~~~~~~~~~~~~~~~~~

"...God opposes the proud but gives grace to the humble..."
James 4:6 (NLT)

Humility is a trigger for God's grace. But what is humility exactly? Well, it's the opposite of being proud, arrogant, egotistical and cocky. It's when you don't have an over-inflated view of yourself. In fact the best definition I've heard for humility is seeing ourselves accurately, as God sees us. God is committed to resist our pride until we see. If He didn't and just let us go, it would show He doesn't really care. But He does, and resists our pride until we turn to Him in humility. We are saying, in effect, I'm willing to get honest about who I am, what I've done and what I want. If we see ourselves in need of God's help and admit it, God pours out grace on us. This grace was bought by Jesus' blood and will do for us whatever we need. If we need salvation, it will save us. If we need deliverance, it will set us free. If we've been wounded, it will heal us. If we walk humbly, we will consistently be able to lay hold of God's supply of grace. He promised and we can count on it.

Prayer Starter: Lord, I humbly ask for grace,

____

____

____

____

in Jesus' name.

PASCAGOULA CATTLE

Dad was a cattle trader who worked five livestock auctions a week for twenty-five years. He also had several men working for him who would attend smaller sales. He annually turned out about a thousand yearlings on native pasture. Sometimes he would buy country cattle. It was not unusual for him to buy an entire herd in a dispersal sale, keep them short-term, and more times than not, sell them at a profit. Sometimes he'd buy a set of bred cows, let 'em calve out, and then sell 'em as pairs.

That's what happened when he bought the Pascagoula cattle. Pascagoula is located on the gulf coast of Mississippi. I have no idea how Dad made the contact or who he bought them from, but he purchased a whole herd of Brahma mother cows off an old man who couldn't take care of 'em anymore. There's lots of low, swampy country down there, and Dad said these cattle came out of the swamps and no one had messed with 'em in a long time. That was an understatement. They were, without question, the wildest, craziest, most ferocious cattle that we ever handled.

They were big, framey cattle, light-colored and all of 'em sported a big rack of horns. A few of the cows already had two-hundred pound calves by their side. The rest were bred and would calve soon. In temperament they would remind you of Mexican fighting bulls. Even the calves would try to run over you. It was nothing for them to leap over a six foot tall board fence. If you were near them on foot you better have your hand on the fence because they would come for you.

Moving them was risky. We had to move them a-horseback even in our barn and adjoining lots because it was the safest way, but even that was a challenge. They'd turn and fight a horse in a heartbeat. If you didn't get out of the way they'd try to run a horn into your horse's underside. One day a big, old cow was able to flip one of our horses and did her best to stomp the cowboy.

Those cattle attacked like they all belonged in a bull-fighters' competition. When the vet came out to test 'em, several died of extreme stress-related trauma. They were as wild as deer and would pile up on each other in a pen if you weren't careful, stomping each other to death.

Dad kept the whole herd for about four months until all of them gave birth to calves. We put them in a pasture across the road and left them alone for awhile, then loaded 'em up and sold them at our local auction.

We talked about the Pascagoula cattle for years. Dad especially enjoyed it when we brought it up to him. One of the last conversations I had with Dad happened when we met at Cracker Barrel for supper. I was in town for a church meeting. We sat down and Dad ordered a T-bone steak, medium. I think

I had fried catfish. No matter. Dad looked good, but older. He wore a nice sport coat and an open collar shirt. I will never forget how he looked as he sat across from me that night.

As we talked, our conversation turned to his many years in the cattle business. We talked about men who worked for Dad- Sidney Joe Davis, Billy Carter, Hollis Mitchell, Dean Parkman, R.C. Holten and others. I didn't say it, but I had actually spent more time with them as a kid than I did with Dad. They were my cowboy heroes.

We talked about horses we used and about his favorite, a buckskin mare we called Dusty. We wondered out loud together if any of those horses were still alive. "Probably not," he said. "If Dusty was still alive she'd be at least twenty-five by now." His eyes twinkled as he talked and he seemed content.

"Do you remember those Pascagoula cattle?", Dad asked.

"I sure do, Dad. How could I ever forget?" We laughed and talked about how wild they were and how hard they were to handle. He shook his head and laughed and laughed, as one memory after another came to mind.

Dad got serious for a moment and said, "And you know, Brad, in spite of all the trouble or the ones that died, we still made a lot of money when we sold those cattle." "Yessir," he said, "we sure did." Though the bunch of wild bovine happened when I was a boy and my dad was a young man, he still remembered the Pascagoula cattle with fondness and laughter.

When I drove away that evening, my mind buzzed with memories. Dad had built a huge cattle business by the time he was forty, owning and leasing thousands of acres. He had bought and sold thousands of cattle and shipped them all over the country. Then, he lost it all and had to start over at the age of forty-two. He went into real estate and sold twenty-eight houses the first month. A year later he bought another ranch and ran cattle till his health forced him to retire.

Dad ended up losing everything he worked for. At the end of his life he was living in a little, shacky house he built himself. It was nothing compared to the fine homes he had built and owned in the past. He had lost more than most will ever have, yet he was happy and very proud of his little place.

It was not long after that night at Cracker Barrel that Dad died. I'm thankful for those memories, not only of the wild cattle, but of that night when Dad and I sat, laughing about the bovine.

The sacrifices we make are the necessary ingredients of a well-lived life. The challenges we face give us the lessons we remember the most. Whatever we've given up or left behind may only be measured accurately when compared to the blessings and benefits we've received. For my Dad, the blessings far outweighed the sacrifices. I feel the same way.

~~~~~~~~~~~~~~~~~~~~~~~~~~~~

"And do not forget to do good and to share with others, for with such sacrifices God is pleased" Hebrews 13:16
~~~~~~~~~~~~~~~~~~~~~~~~~~~~

"PASCAGOULA COWS"

Yonder, over yonder,
How far, was all I thought,
We were out there chasin' cattle,
My old Daddy had just bought.

A herd from Pascagoula,
As wild as any deer,
No way Dad could have known it,
Before they hauled 'em here.

They were big and gray and brahmer,
And one and all had horns,
They weren't scared of the devil,
And there were no forewarns,

That this crazy bunch of cattle,
Would act the way they did,
I can still remember,
Though I was just a kid.

They'd never seen a fence before,
Least that's the way it seemed,
They'd hit it on a full tilt run,
Though our pens were heavy beamed.

And if they could not run through it,
They always tried to jump,
Sometimes they flipped right over,
Landing on their back and rump.

They'd come up all a-snortin',
A pawin' at the ground,
Slobbering on one end,
And green when they turned around.

They'd fight you in a minute,
Whether horseback or on foot,
And you'd best be extra careful,
And quick to not stay put.

When they came a-chargin',
And bellering and all,
You knew they're out to get you,
There was no bluff or stall.

And thankful for the day that came,
When they were loaded up and sold,
Decades passed, I asked my Dad,
If that whole story had been told.

'Bout how wild those cattle were,
That Pascagoula bunch,
He said the old man talked to him,
At the stockyard over lunch.

Daddy said the old man smiled,
When Dad wrote him the check,
Leaned forward in his cane back chair,
Wiped the sweat off of his neck.

Said mister, they are good ones,
But I have to tell you true,
Those cows are on the wild side,
So be careful what you do.

Course Dad was in a hurry,
And always on the go,
Didn't think much of the warning,
We'd handled cows you know.

Dad said as crazy as they were,
And the trouble that they gave,
They still were money makers,
He swore it to the grave.

But let me tell you something,
'Bout a Pascagoula cow,
Don't care how good the deal is,
Find a way to pass somehow.

"They will act religious, but they will reject the power that could make them godly. Stay away from people like that..." **2 Timothy 3:5 (NLT)**

Most of the biblical counsel regarding people is to love them and go try to reach them for Christ. But Paul gives Timothy some startling advice about some folks, and that's to stay away from them. Who are they? They are religious pretenders who deny God's power. Why would Paul say to stay away? In all likelihood it is because these people were not safe. In other words, to expose oneself to them was spiritually dangerous, just like those ferocious cattle from Pascagoula. The best thing is to set a boundary and keep it. Some we have to love and pray for from a distance.

Prayer starter: Lord, help me recognize the ones I am called to reach and those I need to withdraw from,

____

____

____

____

____

____

____

____

____

____

____

____

________________________________in Jesus' name.

*"But may the righteous be glad and rejoice before God;
may they be happy and joyful. Sing to God, sing in praise
of his name, extol him who rides on the clouds ; rejoice
before him—his name is the LORD."*
Psalms 68:3-4 (NIV)

"GOODBYE LARRY MAHAN'

Good-bye, Larry Mahan. Good-bye, Ian Tyson, Don Edwards, Buster Welch, and Baxter Black. Good-bye, Gordon Lightfoot. I even watched the memorial service for Cotton Rosser on the Cowboy Channel the other day. Goodbye Cotton.

My friend, Bubba, called the other day and we talked about Larry Mahan, the cowboy hero. Bubba had stories. He said one time he pulled Larry Mahan's bull rope at the rodeo in Mesquite.

I met Mr. Mahan once, way back in 1982. I had moved back to Texas and had two job possibilities. One was with Nocona boot company and the other selling livestock feed. I drove from Ft. Worth to Dallas for the Nocona interview, and it was there that I ran into Larry Mahan. He was very cordial, and wished me well on my interview. I ended up selling cattle feed in Waco instead of cowboy boots in Vernon.

People live their lives and then we hear that they have crossed over and we remember what they did and said. When I heard that Gordon Lightfoot died I played "If You Could Read My Mind, Love" in the truck, and then heard my friend, Jeff Gore, sing it. Jeff does a great cover.

As a pastor I've been with people in their grief. Some were so devastated by the death of a loved one they could hardly find the strength to go on. This was especially true when we had been praying for a miracle of healing that didn't come. God knows why. Then my Dad died. That was harder, because I had never known a time in my whole life that I couldn't at least pick up the phone and call him. I think of him every day, even though he's been gone twenty years. My brother and I talk about him often, so many things we remember that he said and did. It does not seem real, but it is. Then, my sister tragically died in a drowning accident five years ago. What a shock!

I underestimated how much her death affected me. My brother and I relied on each other, and there was grace for it, but it was very, very hard. Then, my mother was the next to go. And yes, it was a long good-bye because of her dementia. Still, her presence and influence in my life was huge, and I miss her smile and kindness. She mothered me with great tenderness, and I'll always be thankful for her.

When Mom died, my life was changing, but I think I subconsciously thought we were through with death for awhile. Not true. My children's mother died suddenly of Covid-related heart failure in 2021. Our children's hearts were broken and though she's been gone for a while, their grief is still deep.

Paul wrote about this, "...so you will not grieve like people who have no hope." (1 Thess. 4:13 NLT). You see, that's exactly the difference! We do have hope because God gives it to us, and that hope removes the sting of death. Heaven is real. Eternity is what matters most. Always has, always will. Grief is strong, but our hope is stronger.

So yes, now gone are my grandparents on both sides, my parents, my sister, my children's mother, my good friend, Mark, and so many more are gone, too. I don't see how you can be human and not feel the loss. But Jesus is both the resurrection and the life, the author and finisher of our faith, the Alpha and Omega, the beginning and the end, the only Savior, and the great healer of broken hearts. This life is all about the next, and Jesus is Lord of time and eternity. It's a good thing to remember. In Jesus' name, amen.

~~~~~~~~~~~~~~~~~~~~~~~~~

"...you do not even know what will happen tomorrow. What is your life? You are a mist that appears for a little while and then vanishes."
James 4:14 (NIV)
"Man is like a breath; his days are like a passing shadow."
Psalms 144:4 (ESV)
~~~~~~~~~~~~~~~~~~~~~~~~~

DAD'S BELL

It stood right outside Mom's kitchen window beside the driveway. It was an old, heavy cast iron bell that hung, firmly bolted, to a stout creosote post. When I asked Mama what it was for, she said to ring for the neighbors to come if there was a fire. I wasn't supposed to pull it but one day when nobody was lookin', I yanked on the string to ring it and about a thousand yellow jackets stung me before I could get back to the house! Okay, maybe it was only two, but it felt like more. They'd built a big nest in that dern bell and I learned my lesson.

When people came to visit, and back then they would, everyone would park in the driveway by the bell. One time Dad's cousin, Catbird, drove all the way from South Carolina unannounced and stayed two weeks. Church people liked to come on Sunday afternoon. We lived on Todd Road, and you could see people coming for awhile because of the dust flying up from the road less graveled. No matter where they came from, all visitors parked by the bell.

When Dad went bankrupt and lost our home place on Todd Road, we moved to town. The old bell came with us. It was stored away until times got better, and Dad made a new life in the country again. Proudly planted once more, it stood sentinel for many years until life changed and that place had to be sold too. I remember the day Dad took it down. It was a sobering experience.

Dad and Mama later divorced. I was grown. Dad took the bell to his little, shacky built-from-scrap-lumber house and bolted it to a supporting post on the front porch. It didn't hang quite straight, but Dad didn't care. It was still hanging there when he died.

The last time I talked to him in the hospital I asked how he was. He answered, "I'm as weak as a cat." He had a bad heart attack, and the prognosis wasn't good. Linwood had planned to take Dad to Mississippi to live near him, but before he could get Dad out of the hospital, another heart attack happened, and Dad crossed over to Heaven.

When a man's dad dies, something unforeseen happens to him. He feels like everything is up to him now, and he must come of age and be the man. At least that's what happened to me. Even though I had been grown and on my own for a long time, I felt differently about my life somehow, and I asked God to help me get it right.

The funeral was held at a little country church where Dad attended. The preacher told a story about Dad and I'll never forget it. They had built a new building, the one where we sat, and someone had recently given them a large church bell which was mounted to a red brick wall beside the handicapped parking spaces out front. The preacher said that two weeks prior, Dad had come to see him and asked if he could ring the new bell on Sunday mornings to let everyone know the Baptists were having church, and it was time to gather. The preacher agreed and the plan was set but Dad had a heart attack and was gone before they had a chance to ring the bell.

When the preacher finished his story, he signaled to an usher and then said, "We never had the chance to ring the new bell, but we're going to begin right now." The man went outside and, as we listened in silence, he rang the bell eleven times...

My mind ran over with memories. I saw Dad as a young cattleman, and me as a kid holding onto his belt loops as I rode behind him horseback while we checked cattle. I saw him swiftly walking from the barn to the house with his sorting whip under one arm as he studied a big wad of cattle bills in his hands. I saw him dashing to his car on the way to a real estate appointment, fired up about a listing. I saw him in church with a hymnbook in his hand singing his favorite song, "Love Lifted Me."

As the bell tolled, my memories flooded with Dad. I suddenly saw the old bell from my childhood and thought I heard a whisper in my soul. He said: "It's time to ring the bell. Don't wait. Don't put it off. Ring the bell." The message was clear. If you have a song to sing, sing it. If you have a message to write, write it. If you have a word to say, say it. A mission to accomplish? Do it.

Dad didn't leave much behind, but I drove to his little shack, and I took the bell from off his porch. Now, when I look out my window here in the heart of Texas, I can see my Dad's old bell mounted on a post in the yard beside our driveway. It reminds me daily of years past, of Dad, of friends and neighbors, of pain and victories, of dirt roads and life in the country. Mostly, it reminds me that no matter what comes down the road, to always RING THE BELL.

~~~~~~~~~~~~~~~~~~~~~~~~~~~~~~~~~~~~
~~~~~~~~~~~~~~~~~~~~~~~~~~~~~~~~~~~~

BRAD MCCLAIN

"BAXTER BLACK"

"Farewell to Baxter Black"

At the end of every issue of "Western Horseman" magazine there you'd find his words. Baxter Black was always
there. It was most often the thing I read first. What he said,
how he thought, what he wrote and recorded will live on, and
will continue to fill our minds with stories of the cowboy way.
This poem is for him:

Farewell, old friend, farewell,
We're glad you lived to tell,
The stories of the cowboy way,
Adventures in our minds will stay,

For you we ring the bell,
Farewell, old friend, farewell.

You always seemed to speak the lines,
That we were thinking many times,
Good horses, cattle and the fun,
Of crazy wrecks, things we have done,

Authentic stories were the kind,
You always spoke those lines.
We saw how much this nation free,
Meant to you, you helped us see,

The beauty of a place like this,
And freedoms large to never miss,
From out there words of liberty,
You always helped us see.

And from your heart the strong belief,
In God above, His love beneath,
All you said and tried to do,
Showed to Him we must be true,

And now you've found relief,
Because of that belief.
Farewell, old pard, we bid good-bye,
You gave us much, and we will try,

To carry forward all the fun,
With God's help we'll get it done,
And soon we'll join you in the sky,
But for now, we say good-bye.

For you we ring the bell,
Farewell, old friend, farewell.

CHEYENNE

It was my sixtieth birthday and I expected to spend it with family, dinner and a maybe a few presents. I was surprised when an envelope was passed across the table to me. Everyone watched as I opened it and to my great surprise, it contained two tickets to the "Daddy of 'Em All" rodeo in Cheyenne, Wyoming! It was the perfect gift and I knew exactly who was going with me, my brother.

When the time came, Linwood and I drove to Louisiana then flew out of New Orleans to Denver. We were the only hats on the plane. At the Denver airport we picked up a rental car and drove it like we stole it to where we were staying for the week. I had booked a little cabin on the outskirts of Laramie, WY, which was about an hour away from Cheyenne.

We drove up to the cabin and took a minute to look around. It was beautiful. We loved the big wide-open spaces which they called the second largest wind tunnel in the world. The old overland stage route was a few hundred yards from our front porch and the Snow Range Mountains were just to the west. The cabin was small but comfortable and I could hardly sleep that night due to overwhelming excitement. Linwood shared in my excitement.

The next morning I watched the sun come up from the front porch of the cabin. It was forty degrees and the hot cup of coffee in my hand felt good. "Thank You, Lord," I prayed as the prairie turned pink in the pre-dawn light. You could see twenty miles in every direction from that cabin. I could make out several herds of antelope across the plains. A few Angus cattle, looking like little black dots, speckled the pastures in the far distance.

After I finished my coffee, we got cleaned up and headed off to Cheyenne, stopping on the edge of town for a big breakfast- western omelet, of course! The diner was full of cowboys. We nodded to each other, shook hands, told tales and then headed to the rodeo,

When we pulled up to the grounds, we were amazed at the size of the arena and huge grandstands. We ended up watching the rodeo from the end of the arena, standing alongside the fence. It all just seemed unreal to me, and I couldn't believe we were actually there.

During the saddle bronc event, Linwood turned to me and said, "Mark Eagerton is here." We knew he was coming to join us but weren't sure just when. Mark was one of our oldest cowboy buddies from Alabama. When Mark Eagerton arrived anywhere, the party came with him! He was genuinely one of the funniest human beings I've ever known.

Mark didn't take long to find us and it was wonderful to be at Cheyenne with Linwood and Mark. We laughed so much and so hard it made my sides hurt. Even the smile muscles in my face got sore! After the rodeo we went for a steak and then back to the little cabin on the prairie. It was our home that whole week and it's hard to measure the fun we had.

One day we drove west through Centennial, over to the Snowy Mountain range to see the snow in July, quite a sight for Alabama boys. On another day we drove out to Woody Bartlett's ranch near LaGrange, Wyoming. Woody was from our home town, Montgomery, Alabama . He owned ranches near Weatherford, Texas and Wyoming, too. We must have crossed five cattle guards trying to find somebody on this 85,000-acre ponderosa. Jim Peak, also from Alabama, used to run the place, and we got to visit with him for awhile.

The rodeo itself was amazing. There's just so much happening at once you hardly knew which way to look. Trick roping, horseback target shooting, clown shenanigans, trick riding and more were happening the whole time. The extra-long scoring line made all the timed events something to watch, especially the steer wrestling and steer tripping. I'd never been to a rodeo or roping where they had tripping, so we really enjoyed that part. We couldn't help but enjoy the crazy wild horse race at the end of every performance.

Of all the events and all the rides and entertainment, our favorite thing was watching the eight, that's right, eight pickup men do their work. We called 'em the cowboy mafia. They had to rope about every third bull that bucked. Sometimes just one pick-up horse was used to drag 'em out of the arena. Impressive, to say the least.

One night we actually bought tickets to see Jason Aldean in concert. That afternoon a huge storm thundered down both rain and golf ball size hail. The storm turned the arena into a huge mud pit. We took in the concert anyway. Everywhere you looked, there wee young people. We were hock deep in black mud. It didn't take me long to realize I was probably too old to attend any more concerts with people so young, especially in the rain, especially in the mud.

Another memorable moment happened on the Saturday before the final day of the rodeo. The Twombly Horse Sale was held in downtown Cheyenne right in front of the courthouse. They had set up panels to create temporary horse stalls, a big auction ring, and a place for people to sit. We walked around and looked at the horses before the sale began. I guess there were fifty or more for sale and I didn't see one I didn't want. One I remember in particular was a beautiful chocolate palomino gelding, a dream horse for sure. I couldn't tell you his sale price, but whatever it was, it was above my pay grade. I think the lowest-priced animal in the sale was a fourteen-year-old grade buckskin ranch gelding that brought $4,000. We saw a lot of horses go for $20k-plus. I think the top of the sale was close to $100k. The entire sale was really amazing and one of the highlights of the trip.

On Sunday morning we went to the first Cowboy Church service I had ever attended. As we walked in R.W. Hampton was singing "On the Wings of a Snow-White Dove." Cowboys for Christ led the worship service and it was a good one, especially the testimony from a young cowboy who had been badly injured in a horse accident. His parents stood on either side of him, helping to hold him up while he talked. I don't think there was a dry eye in the house.

The final Sunday afternoon performance was memorable. As it progressed, I had the recurring thought that I would never forget that week in Cheyenne. I never have. When it was all finally over, we didn't hang around very long, but drove on back to Laramie. Instead of stopping for supper in Cheyenne, we decided to drive over to the little town of Centennial that we had seen earlier in the week. We thought we'd get a bite to eat at the little bar and grill called "The Friendly."

When we arrived at the grill, there was literally only one person in the place, a lady who told us she was the owner. We chatted for awhile and I boldly told her that If she could find a guitar, my brother would play it. I also assured her he could sing like George Strait. I was half way joking, but she took it to heart.

She disappeared for a few minutes and to our surprise, came back with a guitar! There was a little bandstand over in the corner, and the Alabama boys took the stage. By now a few customers were drifting in. Linwood, Mark and I sang every country song and every gospel tune we knew, one after another till midnight. The Friendly filled to capacity and it looked like all two hundred residents of Centennial, Wyoming showed up. The cowboys from Alabama put an exclamation point on our trip. We had a fun night, and a perfect way to end the week.

I am now 71 and it's hard to believe that our trip to Cheyenne happened over ten years ago. Linwood and I speak of it often. Our friend, Mark, went home to be with the Lord in 2022 and though the three of us frequently talked of returning to Cheyenne, we never were able to get back to that place. Now, the opportunity is gone.

I miss my friend, and I enjoyed going with my brother and Mark. That trip can't be replicated, but the memories linger. I laugh from time to time when I think of the fun times we had in the wide open plains of Wyoming.

In the summer of 2022, I took Stacey to see the "Daddy of 'Em All" and I got to see it through her eyes. That's the last time I've gone. The places we go and the people we love are great blessings from God. I'm glad we didn't miss going to Cheyenne.

Jesus said the thief came to steal, kill and destroy, but that He came to give us abundant life. (John 10:10). In my years around the sun, I've leaned that the abundant life is the great adventure God offers to all of us. It's best not to miss it.

~~~~~~~~~~~~~~~~~~~~~~~~

"The thief comes only to steal and kill and destroy; I came that they may have life, and have it abundantly."
John 10:10 (ESV)

"Every good thing given and every perfect gift is from above, coming down from the Father of lights, with whom there is no variation or shifting shadow."
James 1:17 (NASB)
~~~~~~~~~~~~~~~~~~~~~~~~

"AMIGOS"

When God gives you pards,
Those amigos and friends,
When life's shattered to shards,
Because of back whens.

And they stand side by side,
Like strong trees in a row,
In them you'll confide,
And there so you know,

That God is still with you,
His grace has ahold,
Through friends who are true,
When it's all done and told.

The first was named Linwood,
Then old Bart, Gayle, and Brad,
There's Jeff and yes, Kevin,
Bub and Russ, friends I've had.

There's Bruce and there's Tyson,
My friends old and new,
There's Robert and Richard,
Top hands through and through.

There are many more brothers,
Such as Mark, who stood by me,
Mentors, gone to heaven,
From my past, don't you see.

And they've made the difference
In the man that I am,
And stood strong with me,
When I was in a jam.

So thank God when He gives you,
Those who sharpen and stay,
So you keep on going,
And so you'll be okay.

"Two people are better off than one, for they can help each other succeed. If one person falls, the other can reach out and help. But someone who falls alone is in real trouble."
Ecclesiastes 4:9-10 (ESV)

God is not calling lone rangers. He is putting together a posse. We are called into spiritual relationships of support and accountability. From these we receive both encouragement and adjustment. We do not do very well if we isolate ourselves and try to fight our battles alone. It's where two or three are gathered that we can expect the presence of the Lord in special ways. If you do not have at least two or three friends standing with you, it should be the next thing you ask the Lord to do in your life.

Prayer Starter: Lord, give me partners, true friends I can count on,

____

____

____

____

____

____

—

, in Jesus' name.

OWYHEE

John Babb. He was the friend of a friend, that's all. "You should call him sometime," my friend Jeff said. "I think y'all would really get along," he added. I didn't think a whole lot about it, pro or con, and calling a stranger, albeit with an invitation, was not too high on my "to do" list. But eventually the call was made and almost immediately, a close connection.

John was the pastor of a church way off up yonder in Twin Falls, Idaho. He might as well have been a missionary to a foreign country. Turns out he was from South Carolina and educated in Texas. My Dad's people were from South Carolina, and I finished college in Texas, so we had that in common. He had a deep, gravelly voice on the phone, a dry wit, and a plainspoken way about him that I immediately liked.

Through the months we talked about once a week, and whether the subject was horses or cattle or church or a Bible passage, we covered lots of bases. I came to trust his words and appreciated his encouragement. I will say that I've learned many hard lessons in the friendship department. I have been so wounded as a man that I trusted people who appeared to be friends but turned out not to be. If you find enough of that kind, you get gun-shy about trusting anybody at all. But it didn't take me long to know that John Babb was the real deal.

John and his wife, Carmen, built a little cottage on their place to host people who need a spiritual break. John talked with me about this and invited me to come up there and spend a few days. If I came, he said, I would be welcome to go with him on his riding job for a large ranch in that area. When he said large, I had no idea what he meant, but turns out the outfit was approximately sixty miles long and an average of fifteen miles wide! It was owned by fifth generation ranchers, and they also ran their 6,000-plus cattle herd on grass leases across the state line in Nevada.

It was there at the Owhyee desert country at the top of the Great Basin, where John laughingly said livestock made a living going twelve miles an hour. "Come, spend some time up here with me," he said at the end of every phone conversation. Sounded good, but I didn't think I'd ever do it. One day my wife said she thought it would be great if I took the time to go. But that's always it, isn't it? Finding the time and feeling like it's okay to step away and put everything on hold for a week. But somehow, surprisingly, it all worked out.

I planned the dates in September, purchased the plane tickets and headed to Idaho. The weather was amazing. In September in Texas, it's still hot and summer still lingers in the air. 100 degree temps still scorch the days and the nights are just as warm. But in Idaho it would get down into the thirties at night and never got above about seventy-five during the day. It was delightful!

John and Carmen were gracious hosts and got me all settled down in their clean, comfortable, well-stocked cottage across from their home. It was a pleasure. After early morning coffee, John and I were up and gone before dawn, with horses saddled and loaded, headed from his house out to the ranch an hour away. As the sun rose slowly over that vast, broken country, John talked to me of spiritual things. I was moved by his words. Time and again, he spoke of things that matter most to men who love the Lord and the land.

He knew some of my personal history and told me it would probably take a couple of days, but if I listened, the desert would speak to me. I didn't understand what he was talking about. He said, "The Lord is everywhere, but in this remote place, you can hear Him better." I thought of the times Jesus took His disciples aside to lonely, desert places. John was right.

All day each day for five days we were in the saddle. And, as Gus McRae said, "Ain't nothing better than riding a fine horse through a new country." John's horses were solid and knew the country, even though I was surprised by some of the steep trails we took. One day we rode up and over the White Elephant mountains, and that one was memorable.

Every day we moved cattle. John would point and say, "Brad, do you see those cattle down there?"

"No, John I don't see any cattle."

"Look where I'm pointing? Do you see 'em now?" My dad used to say those exact words to me. "Look where I'm pointing". To any avail, I would strain my eyes, looking across the vast landscape and after great concentration, I would see tiny black specks on the distant horizon.

"I think I see 'em, John."

"Okay, you move those this way, and as you go, if you pick up other bunches just keep 'em moving in this direction. I'll meet back up with you in about an hour or so."

"Yessir," and off I rode. I went one way and John went another. It might take forty-five minutes at a long trot to even get close enough to see how many cows there were in the bunch, but then I'd ease around 'em and get 'em moving. We did this everyday, over some of the roughest country I ever saw. It was great cowboy fun, and I tried to take mental snapshots of all of it.

Every day was a pattern. John's devotional talks in the morning, move cattle all day, fellowship on the way back, then have supper with John and Carmen each night. I enjoyed the routine.

The week was not without comedy. John had given me grief all week about wearing pearl snap cowboy shirts versus the plain, generic work shirts he deemed more appropriate for cowboy work. He said my pearl snaps were my "cowboy costume," and kidded me about it without mercy.

One day early afternoon we rode up on a large concrete watering trough, the kind they used all over the ranch. It had a steel pipe welded across the top to keep calves out but somehow a pretty good-sized yearling had gotten into the trough. He was splashing around in dark green water, and John stepped off his horse and handed me his reins. "Hold my horse here for a minute, if you would," he said.

"Do you need my help?" I asked.

"Don't think so," he gruffly responded. I laughed as he stood, pondering at the disaster in front of us.

He walked closer to the trough, trying to figure out a way to somehow get the calf out. In the process, the yearling kicked green water all over John. He was covered in it from head to toe. After a little while of pondering over the unyielding mess, he said someone else would have to be sent back to get the calf out. Now dripping with green, smelly water, he walked back towards me and I handed him the reins.

As he stepped back on his big roan gelding, I broke silence and told him, "You know, John, if you had been wearing a pearl snap shirt that calf wouldn't have kicked green all over you." He didn't think it was too funny but I was amused. I quietly laughed as we rode off.

On a couple of evenings after supper John sat down at the piano in his living room and played old hymns while I listened and cried. We worshipped together and starting on the third day I began to hear the Lord say things to me I needed to hear.

I suppose it took that long for the noise inside of me to quiet down enough to hear the "voice" in the wind. Everything the Spirit said had something to do with being completely free of the need to please men and to be completely devoted to pleasing the Lord. It meant having no other agenda other than what He assigns, and no other endorsement beyond His own. One distinctive word was, "If I am your Advocate, you need no other." Humbling, to say the least.

I'll never forget my time in the Owyhee Desert with my good friend, John Babb. God's vast creation, God's voice, and the man sent by God to be my friend made the time memorable. In every way possible, He restored my soul on that trip. If you get the chance to draw aside, take it. I know, life is busy, but to be still and know that He is God will do you a world of good.

~~~~~~~~~~~~~~~~~~~~~~~~

"Be still, and know that I am God..."
Psalm 46:10 (ESV)

"Be still before the Lord and wait patiently for Him..."
Psalm 37:7 (NIV)

"For God alone, O my soul, wait in silence, for my hope is from Him."
Psalm 62:5 (ESV)
~~~~~~~~~~~~~~~~~~~~~~~~

"AUTHENTIC"

Soon the day is coming,
When you finally decide,
If you will be authentic,
Or from Jesus hide.

You've tried to please the others,
You worked to get their smile,
You changed your plans to suit 'em,
You've gone the extra mile.

And had good intentions,
Keep peace and get along,
Btu when you did the best you could,
You still did not belong.

To the club that they insisted,
Was where you ought to be,
And the price of their admission,
Was just too high you see.

The Lord gave you salvation,
He gave you special gifts,
You have the Holy Spirit,
Through you folks' burden lifts.

But the cowboy way you've wanted,
Is in your DNA,
And you know God will use it,
And He has shown the way.

For you to be authentic,
Just be who you are,
Surrender all to Jesus,
You trust His grace so far.

And He will not forsake you,
Just learn to cowboy up,
Be the man He made you,
And let Him fill your cup.

~~~~~~~~~~~~~~~~~~~~~~~~~~~~~~~~~
~~~~~~~~~~~~~~~~~~~~~~~~~~~~~~~~~

"He restores my soul. He leads me in the paths of righteous-
ness for His name's sake."
Psalm 23:3 (ESV)

The twenty-third Psalm is perhaps the most well-loved psalm of all. It is beautiful, and describes our relationship with God our Shepherd. Much later Jesus described Himself as the Good Shepherd who lays down His life for the sheep. The psalm is all about coming home to ourselves as those who are cared for by God. He restores us to our true selves, heals us of the frantic stress of trying to be someone or something other that who we are. Being led on paths of righteousness means we learn to cooperate with the identity God wants us to have, made secure by Him. We are His sheep and He the One who gets to define us and discipline us from false and selfish identities that compete with God's best. He fills our cup to overflowing and promises eternal companionship. There is no better way to live.

Prayer Starter; Lord, help me wholeheartedly receive You as my Shepherd,

____

____

____

____

____in Jesus' name.

THE NEIGHBOR'S BULL

Linwood called me and said his neighbor's bull was out again. She was an old grandmother who couldn't keep her fences in very good repair, and the young bull she bought just wouldn't stay home. There was a cow herd down the road and that's where he always went. He was a four year old Brangus and weighed about a thousand pounds. We wanted to help the woman, plus we were always up for a cowboy adventure. We saddled our horses and rode over to the place, not far from Linwood's house.

We figured we would ride out to find the bull and drive him out into the road and back to the pasture where he belonged. Simple, right? Well, we hoped so, and at first things went pretty well. It was the fall of the year if I remember right, so the hottest days were over and there was a nice breeze that afternoon. We were in good spirits. I was riding my gray quarter horse, Drifter. I had bought him in Ft. Worth and he was a good one. Linwood, was riding his pretty sorrel mare, Penny. She was well-built and flashy, with a white blaze and four white stockings. Everywhere he took that horse people wanted to buy her.

We opened the gate on the road and let ourselves into the pasture. I don't remember who owned that place and I assumed Linwood's neighbor had called to let them know we were coming. No one lived there and there was no one around. The pasture was open in the front with woods in the back of the property, and that's where we found the bull. We cut him out of the cow herd and pushed him slowly back toward the road. Sometimes cattle do better if you drive several along with the one you really want. That might have been a better strategy, but the bull didn't give us any trouble. We quietly and slowly drove him out of the woods and toward the front of the property. I eased ahead and opened the gate, then back to where Linwood held the bull. We pushed him toward it, and that's when he made his move. Instead of the right direction, all of a sudden he angled at a dead run back toward the cattle. We couldn't turn him and he got away.

"Well, dang," Linwood said. "I sure wish we could have gotten him on the first pass." I agreed. It's always better if you can get it done the first time, with as little noise and stress as possible.

"Let's just give him another try," I said. We didn't rush, but walked the horses back to where we had found the bull the first time. Sure enough, there he was with the cows again. This time we took a couple of cows along with him, and easily enough, drove them slowly out of the woods and into the open ground in the front. This was about twenty acres large, so again I went ahead and opened the gate while Linwood held the cattle.

We moved them toward the gate, and I'll be derned if that fool didn't do the same thing again. It didn't matter that we had a couple of cows with him. He turned back toward the woods and made a rush to get away. We thought there's no way he'll beat us to the woods, but no amount of horsemanship could make him turn. He took the two cows with him and was gone into the brush.

"That's it!" Linwood said. "We are going to rope this bull." I grinned. It's actually what I hoped we would do from the beginning. "Let's get around him one more time.", Linwood hollered. "This time when he makes his move, we'll get him caught and lead him home."

"I'll be ready," I promised.

We both stepped off the horses and tightened our cinches a notch. I took down my rope, made a loop and twirled it a time or two, then put it back in place. "Let's get him," Linwood said, and off we went. This time we long trotted to the back, and didn't slow down till we got the bull located. He made no attempt to escape, and moved right off when we pushed him along. We didn't bother bringing other cows this time, feeling like they might just be in the way when we started to rope him.

Slowly we drove him through the brush. He'd stop and take a bite of grass, then walk along, never very far ahead of us. In about thirty minutes we had him out of the woods and into open ground. There was sage and bushes here and there and a few places where weeds were fairly tall, but it shouldn't be too much trouble to get a rope on him.

What we planned was for one of us to catch him with a head loop and the other ride in and heel him. Once we got him laid down, we could then halter him with both ropes on his head and lead him out together. That was the plan, anyway. I rode around again and opened the gate.

We took down our ropes and made loops so we would be ready when he turned back. We drove him a little further, and for a moment, it looked like he was going to surprise us and allow us to drive him out through the gate. But then all of a sudden he threw his tail in the air and made his move. Just like before, he angled at a dead run back for the woods. This time we let him come and made no attempt to turn him. He was closer to me than Linwood so I got ready to take the first shot.

I spurred Drifter up into a gallop and there we went, jumping weeds and dodging bushes as we pursued the bull. I began twirling my loop above my head as the bull approached at an angle. This time I was going to simply fall in behind him and put it on him. Here he came, and I knew in a second I was going to get him caught. Just as I was about to make my throw, something terrible happened. I found myself driven into the ground! It was like Drifter just went right out from under me going forward and fell down and sideways onto my leg. It happened so fast the front of my hat was crushed into the ground and my lips hit the briars.

Dazed, I looked up to see Drifter's head right next to mine and hear the bull snorting as he kept on running. Drifter struggled and then got up, reins hanging down. He started grazing and seemed okay. I didn't get up. I couldn't. I had the breath knocked out of me and it felt like my ankle was broken.

Linwood came trotting up and was laughing. "I wish there was some way we could have filmed that," he said. "Are you okay?"

When I could talk I said, "No, I don't think so," as I sat there rubbing my leg. I pulled off my boot and sock, and my ankle was turning colors. In a little while we got back on the horses and rode on home. Catching that bull would have to wait.

Turns out Drifter had hit a little piece of leftover cross fence that was grown over but still strong enough to cause him to stumble that day. My ankle was bruised but not broken, along with my pride. The next week the neighbor tolled her bull back home with feed, and without the help of top hands like us. Good thing.

I'll never forget the day the neighbor's bull got out and we almost caught it. Some of the best stories in life don't end the way you imagine, but it's good that they happen anyway. Sometimes you get what you go for, and sometimes not, but it really isn't always the result that matters the most, it's the try. So, no matter if you catch what you aim for, what's important is that you do it from the heart.

" Whatever you do, work heartily, as for the Lord and not for men, knowing that from the Lord you will receive the inheritance as your reward. You are serving the Lord Christ." Colossians 3:23-24 (ESV)

"STUMBLE"

___

My old pony had a stumble,
Coming down a real steep place,
He kept on a-goin',
And soon regained his pace.

He's a darn sure-footed pony,
Only once or twice gone down,
This was just a little stumble,
Whilst making our big round.

I thought how I have stumbled,
Along life's rocky path,
I thought of times I've fallen,
And wondered if God's wrath,

Would somehow be the end result,
Of what I've said and done,
He'd judge me and reject me,
When my race soon gets run.

No sooner that I thought it,
It occurred to me,
That though my horse has stumbled,
He's still my favorite, see.

And I do not reject him,
Just 'cause of times he fell,
I still want to keep him,
I do not want to sell.

The Lord said in a small way,
I hope you understand,
That though you're far from perfect,
Your life is in my hand.

I love you and won't judge you,
My Son has paid your price,
For every single stumble,
My grace for you suffice.

And when I see you stumble,
I'll steady you along,
And when you fall and hit the ground,
Forgive and right the wrong.

So when you make your circle,
And the trail gets rough and steep,
My grace is there to help you,
So do your best to keep,

Your gaze on looking forward,
Yes, focus on the prize,
I am right beside you,
You're special in My eyes.

~~~~~~~~~~~~~~~~~~~~~~~~~

"Look straight ahead, and fix your eyes on what lies before you..."
Proverbs 4:25 (NLT)

Focus is a huge component of anyone's success. If we lack focus as believers in Jesus Christ, we will easily be distracted by the noisy sales pitch of the world. You've probably heard the story of the little girl whose mother offered to buy her one toy of her choosing, but only one. She had a hard time deciding, but finally chose a doll she liked. When they turned to go to the check-out counter, the little girl asked her mother to blind-fold her so she wouldn't be distracted by other choices! Jesus spoke of seeking God's kingdom as our highest priority, and not allowing worry to torment us. Simon was able to walk on the waves as long as he focused on Jesus. Paul talked about forgetting the past and pressing on to win the heavenly prize. The writer of Hebrews encourages looking to Jesus, the author and finisher of our faith. Focus can keep us on track, and if we stumble or fall, help us to recover quickly.

Prayer Starter: Lord, help me to stay focused on You and all that really matters,

____

____

in Jesus' name.
~~~~~~~~~~~~~~~~~~~~~~~~~

LAST RIDE

A whole way of life was coming to an end, and I knew it. For a very long time, home was the ranch in Hope Hull. Obviously not the place where I was raised, mind you, because Mom and Dad bought it about the time I left for college. No matter, it was home to all of us. It was beautiful, with rolling pastures, big shade trees, and a couple of nice ponds. Dad built onto the original ranch house, and people felt welcomed there. Mom called it "Heaven's Gate" and for many people that's exactly what it was.

People gathered there for a Bible study or to sit at my mother's table or to just have a soft place to land. Strangers came and didn't want to leave. I can't say how many young people prayed to receive the Lord at that kitchen table. A thousand memories- of pastures full of yearlings, team roping, bird hunts, family gatherings, prayers, tears, laughter and music. And now it was ending.

Life changed. Dad got sick. Everything shifted and the place had to be sold, parcel by parcel. Now, it was down to the house and a few acres. Before I knew it, they had a contract to sell the last piece of dirt and the house we called home.

I was living in Pensacola, Florida, pastoring a church at that time. Call me nostalgic, but I decided I needed to ride the home ranch one more time. Whether or not he would remember it, I wanted my little boy, Tristan, to ride it with me.

We always tried to keep a couple of horses at that time, and I had given the kids a Welsh pony for Christmas. I called Mom and told her we were coming and she, as always, was so excited. We got up early the very next day and loaded the horses.

Back then I rode a buckskin paint mare I named Dove, and she turned out to be a better buggy than saddle horse. No matter, she'd do for this ride. The Welsh pony was also a mare, a pretty bay with a negative disposition. You might say she was "marish."

It was an easy three hour drive, and Mom ran out to meet us when we pulled into the driveway. She already had lunch ready even though it was only 10:00 AM. Then again, lunch was always ready at "Heaven's Gate."

She spooned up a big steaming bowl of vegetable beef stew and with it, an oversized wedge of the best corn bread you ever put in your mouth. She even had a freshly baked caramel cake for dessert. We ate with her and then headed out.

I had to take down the wire so our horses could step across. Tristan asked me if what we were doing was okay. He was only five years old at the time. I said it was totally fine, even though we were technically trespassing. If I could have cared less, I don't see how. Off we went.

As we passed through, I told stories to Tristan. He had heard before, but this is where they actually happened. "This little slope right here is where your Uncle Linwood and I were riding along when that colt we named "Cotton-eyed Joe" bucked me off. One moment we were walking along just like we are today, slack-reined and talking, and the next moment I was on the ground. Joe pitched me right over his head. Your Uncle Linwood thought it was real funny."

"When your Poppa 'Clain first bought this place, this bottom was all grown up and cattle from our neighbor came back and forth across the creek. I once penned a dozen head just as it got dark, and roped one that turned back and dragged him in." We rode on and he asked for more stories.

"Tell me about the big flood," he said with excitement.

"That year it rained so much that Pintlala Creek got way out of its banks and flooded this whole back pasture. See that little knoll right there with the three pine trees?"

He said, "Yessir, I see it."

"There were about twenty-five yearlings cut off on that hill surrounded by water", I told him. I could remember like it was yesterday. "When we went to get 'em, the horses had to swim across and we had to swim the cattle out. It was the first time I ever rode a swimming horse."

"Did any of 'em drown?", he asked.

"Not that day," I softly answered.

And so it went, story after story, until the sun started dropping over the pastures. I knew we needed to turn back. I had been leading the pony the whole time with a lead rope, while Tristan held his own reins. When we turned, for some reason she pitched and Tristan fell off. Derned pony. He wasn't hurt, and we rode on in with one more story to tell.

I can't help but think that life bucks you off sometimes. When it does, all you can do is step back on and keep riding. That's what we did that day. As we loaded up the mares and headed back, Tristan fell asleep in the truck. His little face dirty from the ride and fall. He slept peacefully next to me none the less. I glanced over at Tristan. I looked up at the beautiful sky above me. I thought of this last ride across my old home place. Hope Hull was in my rear view mirror as I headed for Florida. A reminder that you often have to say good-bye to what WAS so you can get ready for what IS ABOUT TO BE.

"Brothers and sisters, I know that I have not yet reached that goal, but there is one thing I always do. Forgetting the past and straining toward what is ahead, I keep trying to reach the goal and get the prize for which God called me through Christ to the life above."
Philippians 3:13-14 (NCV)

"LEAVING"

A lot of life is leaving,
Hellos and then good-byes,
Joy and lots of laughter,
And times we have our cry's.

'Cause babies don't stay babies,
They grow up and move away,
And every time it happens,
You bow your head and pray,

That they will find someone to love,
And life that's blessed and sweet,
Chase their dreams, do what it takes,
To overcome defeat.

The grandkids, you remember,
Are growing like a weed,
So do your best to love on them,
And give them what they need.

'Cause very soon they too will go,
Surprise you with good-bye,
To go and live out of the nest,
You pray for all their try.

People whom you counted on,
Decide to move away,
Some don't even stay in touch,
But you learn to be okay.

'Cause some were never with you,
Even though you thought they were,
And either way it's in His hands,
Though not what you'd prefer.

We say good-bye to those who die,
Though they leave an empty space,
That only the Good Lord can fill,
With His amazing grace.

And in the end we say good-bye,
To this old life and world,
Go through the gates of splendor,
God's banner then unfurled.

The gift of life eternal,
Is what this life's about,
And when we say good-bye for good,
His face we'll see, no doubt.

"I have written this to you who believe in the name of the Son of God, so that you may know you have eternal life..." (1 John 5:13, NLT)

We all have to say our good-byes, but when this life is finally over, we believe in eternal life. These words from John the apostle bring great comfort to us. He writes so that we may know we have eternal life. What he is saying is that this should not be a "hope-so," "think-so," or "maybe-so" kind of thing. This should be something that we know is true, giving us an assurance and confidence when we face death.

There are far too many people who struggle with this issue, when God wants to give them peace about it. It's a huge part of our inheritance as God's children. Let the Lord make you sure.

Prayer Starter: Lord, please give us assurance that we have received eternal life,

____

____

____

____

____

____

____

____

____

in Jesus' name.

Linwood (left) and Brad (right)
SLE Rodeo - 2022

"So do not fear, for I am with you; do not be dismayed, for I am your God. I will strengthen you and help you; I will uphold you with my righteous right hand." **Isaiah 41:10 (NIV)**

EMU

My friend, Brad Moore, got the call from a neighbor. The neighbor told Brad that his emu had escaped and that it was in the pasture with Brad's cows. He asked Brad if he thought he could herd him into the catch pen and hold him until they could come to get him. My friend assured him we'd get it taken care of and call him later. We had planned a trail ride that day, so Brad figured we could herd the emu and get it penned by noon.

"Okay, thanks so much," the neighbor said. They both hung up and Brad immediately wondered how much trouble it would be to herd the bird. He'd gathered cattle his whole life, caught wild ones when necessary and was an experienced hand. Though he was a great cow hand, he'd never fooled with an emu or anything close. I don't expect many cowboys have.

It was a warm, spring day, and he hoped the horses didn't get too hot when it came time to go after that thing. The riders showed up in a little while. Several teenage girls had come to ride, and our old friend, Bart. Bart unloaded his little jenny mule, Darla. Darla was as pretty as a picture. She was dappled brown with a flax mane and tail and barely stood fourteen hands. Bart could do anything with Darla, as broke as a mule can be. The girls were experienced riders. Brad called the group together when everyone was cinched up and mounted. "The first thing we need to do today is gather an emu that's gotten into my pasture up the road. We'll just ease around the thing and see if we can't push him into the catch pen without too much fuss." Everyone sat there sort of surprised, but Bart was the most excited. "This is gonna be good," he thought. Off they all went.

When they opened the gate at the pasture up the road, it was one of those perfect spring days that makes you glad to be alive. A soft breeze was blowing, the grass was lush because the rain had been good, and the cattle were fat with frisky calves by their sides. But no one saw the emu. "We'll just ease around this way," Brad said, as he pointed them all to the left. We'll make a circle and see if we can't locate this escapee." The riders moved off at a walk. Brad was in the lead on his little red roan gelding he called "Rojo." The three girls were in the middle, and Bart brought up the rear of the group.

There was a small pond and a little bunch of woods up ahead, and Brad thought maybe the emu was hiding there. As they moved through the edge of the woods, the fence was on their left and the pond on their right. They heard something moving ahead of them, and all of the sudden the emu burst out of the woods running straight toward them. What happened next should have been caught on video, 'cause things got pretty western.

One of the girl's horses broke in half bucking and pitched her over the fence! She landed hard and decided to lay there awhile. Her horse ran off. The other two girls' horses were both running sideways, as was Brad's horse, Rojo. One of girls' horses ran sideways into the pond and she fell off in the water. Brad got Rojo turned but he didn't want to face the monster. But the worst one was Darla.

Without wasting a second, Darla whirled and headed back to the barn at a full gallop. Bart pulled so hard on the reins he broke her curb strap, and then the race was on. The further she ran, the faster she went, and all Bart could do was hold on. He had her head turned all the way to the side but it didn't matter. She was leaving the country no matter what he did!

Meanwhile the emu swerved off and the last time anyone saw, was headed back into the woods. No one could say if the emu meant to attack them, but we all doubt it. Emu's don't attack. Brad rode to help the girl who fell off across the fence, while the other two girls got their horses calmed down. But not Darla. She was still running and heading for a tall fence with barbed wire at the top. Bart had never imagined she might run through a fence, but he took no chances.

At the last possible moment, he bailed off to the left, and Darla came to a sliding stop before hitting the fence. She stood there, snorting with reins trailing, when Bart caught her and fashioned a new curb strap out of bailing twine. Then he stepped back on and went to find the others.

The rest of the group had had enough for the day. The one girl had sprained or maybe broken her wrist when she fell, but that was the only injury. A few days later they managed to lure the emu into the catch pen with feed, and that was the end of the story. Hoping for the best but being ready for the worst is part of the cowboy code.

James wrote we should count it all joy when we run into trials. This may be true, though I'm not sure James ever had to deal with a wild emu.

~~~~~~~~~~~~~~~~~~~~~~~~~~~
~~~~~~~~~~~~~~~~~~~~~~~~~~~

"EMU "

I stood up in my stirrups,
Just so I could see,
The strangest bird I ever saw,
Looking back at me.

It was a big old emu,
And one some neighbor had,
He jumped o'er all the fences,
Man, that bird was bad.

They sent us out to pen him,
Didn't say just how,
And when our ponies saw him,
They lost their minds right now.

Some, they went to buckin',
Bart's mule ran away,
He barely got old Darla,
Reined back in that day.

Tried so hard to turn her,
Broke her old chin strap,
Cut a piece of hay string,
And shook out his old chap.

Meanwhile went the emu,
Like a fire on it had set,
I never knew those devils,
Could run that fast and yet,

Somehow we got around him,
Started the right way,
And that's the last we saw him,
That's all I have to say.

Love to claim I roped him,
But that would not be true,
Love to say Moore heeled him,
But neither did he do.

So what happened to that chicken,
We tried to pen that day,
Last seen two counties over,
And for me that's okay.

I'll stick to penning cattle,
And roping steers sometime,
I'll drag calves to the fire,
And cowboy up just fine.

But some things are just better,
If we leave them alone,
And that includes the emus,
I hope they all stay home.

~~~~~~~~~~~~~~~~~~~~~~~~~~

"How can light live with darkness?" **(2 Cor. 6:14, NLT)**

Sometimes we have to draw the line in our relationships. We are called to love everyone, live at peace, forgive all those who hurt us, and be a witness as much as possible. People who don't know the Lord need love, and we're the ones to give it. But, there are times when it's just not safe to be around somebody. Perhaps they are a bad influence on us, or a temptation, or just don't want to change. If we put ourselves at risk in the name of love, we are defeating God's purpose for them and for us. That's why this scripture asks the question how can light live with darkness? The question implies this reality: who is influencing who, in this situation? And if the darkness is winning it's time to withdraw. Think about it. God will show you how.

Prayer Starter: Lord, help us to recognize Your boundaries,,,

____

____

____

____

____

____

____________________________, in Jesus' name.
~~~~~~~~~~~~~~~~~~~~~~~~~~

"Let your speech always be gracious, seasoned with salt, so that you may know how you ought to answer each person."
Colossians 4:6 (ESV)

LONGHORNS

About twenty some odd years ago my brother, Linwood, gave me a belt buckle with the head and horns of a longhorn on it. It wasn't very large and I really liked it, wearing it off and on through the years. Eventually, however, it got boxed up in a move and I forgot about it. Time passed and my life changed dramatically.

After years of marriage, my life changed and I found myself divorced. I moved out of my home and moved into an apartment over a buddy's barn. Gayle Young was a good cowboy friend of mine and he helped me by giving me a place to be. Though I left everything I had spent years building, I found that my new chapter let me get back to my cowboy roots.

I was by myself in a little rustic barn attic apartment, and while many would have been depressed about the life shift, I found myself spending more time with my horses than I had been able to do in a very long time and that felt good. I felt like I had come home to myself. For the first time in a long time, I felt like me.

Gayle had a beautiful place out in the country. He had several acres, beautiful pastures with a creek running along the edge. My horses grazed the meadows along the creek bed and I found great joy in watching them. He had a large lighted arena and round pens. From my little apartment I could see the round pens and the pastures beyond. Right behind the barn were the pens and the working chute where he once kept longhorn cattle.

I met Stacey, a Texas woman, while I was living in that little barn. I fell in love with her. We ran off to the Working Ranch Cowboy Finals Rodeo in Amarillo, TX and got married in the fall of the year. Jeff Gore, a cowboy, musician, preacher, and my friend, married us and I will be forever grateful. His wife, Donna, promised to always keep us in their prayers. She meant it. When we left Amarillo that weekend, we knew we needed to decide on a place to live. I knew she shouldn't live in that little barn. Stacey and I talked about living in Alabama for about fifteen seconds before we quickly knew that Texas would be our home.

We bought a small place on the outskirts of Weatherford. David Mangold gave me my first job in Texas, as a drover for the city of Fort Worth's longhorn herd. "The Herd," as it is called, is driven twice a day down Exchange Avenue in the historic Stockyard District.

The famous Fort Worth street is closed to vehicular traffic and the sidewalks are lined with people from all over the world who gather to see those big, old steers walking down the brick-covered thoroughfare. This is reminiscent of when thousands of longhorn cattle were driven from south Texas through Fort Worth before their journey north over the old Chisholm Trail to the railheads in Kansas. The slow meandering of the Long-horns and the loud call of the drovers on the streets of Fort Worth gives folks a twice-a-day taste of "what once was".

For a year I worked three days a week as part of that horseback crew and really enjoyed it. I wore my 1800 cowboy clothing; wide brimmed felt hat, high top boots, leather cuffs, canvas pants and cotton shirts. I loved my job. I was horse back. I worked with cattle. I even met people from nearly every state and from many foreign countries. I did it all in the historic streets of Fort Worth, TX. What an adventure.

Some of those big old steers weigh over a ton and have horn spans of seven feet! Some might think it was an easy task to drive those cattle, since they were pretty docile and broken to the daily route. Almost all the time that is true but there's always that one day out of a hundred that some steer would wander off course or a runaway child or a barking dog would cause a moment of panic.

Once, on a day when the temperature was dropping rapidly, we drove the cattle across the parking lot for the afternoon drive. On this occasion they turned back toward us, galloping past us towards their corral. Three of the old-man-broke herd horses saw the galloping herd and immediately tried to buck us off! We all held our seat, but it proves that things can still get western in old Fort Worth!

While working at The Herd I met a fellow named Russell Fairchild. Russell came to coach us from time to time on handling the big steers. He was a long-time longhorn owner and consultant, and was always very helpful to us. One day I noticed a Facebook post from Russell advertising a registered longhorn bull for sale. We talked on the phone, and the following week, Stacey and I drove to Russell's ranch near Lampasas, Texas to pick up the bull and three longhorn heifers. We brought them home, turned them out on our pastures.

We've built new fences, developed pastures, added temporary catch pens, and built a life here with our own herd. Our first calf was born in August of 2023, a pretty little bull calf. Now, in a small way, we own a piece of Texas history and get to enjoy these colorful and magnificent cattle every single day.

The other day, I pulled a small box from the back of a drawer, and there was my old longhorn buckle. I fastened it to an old belt I had bought at the Summerdale Saddle Shop near Robertsdale, Alabama. The silver conchos on the belt matched the longhorn buckle perfectly.

I could not help but think of all that has happened since my brother gave it to me so many years ago. What's even better than finding the old buckle is actually owning and being able to take care of the longhorn cattle whose head and horns now grace the belt. Psalm 50:10 says: "For every animal of the forest is Mine, and the cattle on a thousand hills." If God owns so many, there's no doubt in my mind that some of them have long horns. I figure if I can take care of them and He can take care of them, He can definitely take care of us.

~~~~~~~~~~~~~~~~~~~~~~~~~~~~
~~~~~~~~~~~~~~~~~~~~~~~~~~~~

"A COWBOY THEN"

We didn't know it was a story,
That someday they would tell,
Just felt like work, we didn't shirk,
Uphill to ring the bell.

And all the cowboy romance,
Plumb wasted on us hands,
As Dad would say, it's work, not play,
In a hurry with his plans.

Didn't care if you enjoyed it,
Suspicious if you did,
From can till can't, but now they paint,
With manure and sweat all hid.

The glory of the cowboy,
A-horseback through the brush,
Full out to find, the wild bovine,
Fast gallop in a rush.

But then when working at it,
With sweat and blood and tears,
No glory there, gave all, I swear,
Said no to all our fears.

Fondly now I see and hear,
All those cowboy days,
And what I'd give, to go relive,
I'll treasure them always.

But back when it was happening,
Spite of laughter and the fun,
We earned our pay and everyday,
We rode to get it done.

Endured and kept on going,
'Cause that's just what we did,
No thought about, or cause for doubt,
That one day they'd get rid,

Of all the open spaces,
We rode so carelessly,
With stockyards closed, in still repose,
Of runs that used to be.

You can't go back, they say it,
And wrong if you belong,
To yesterday, the price you pay,
Is sadness you prolong.

But I've still got my memories,
Still catch a horse and ride,
The life goes on, more brain, less brawn,
If they said I'm done, they lied.

The story of a cowboy,
Has no end, you see,
When cows need care, he will be there,
And it will always be.

~~~~~~~~~~~~~~~~~~~~~~~~~~

"...I own the cattle on a thousand hills..."
Psalm 50:10 (NLT)

There is romance embedded in the cowboy way. The same is true with all sorts of human endeavors- sea voyages, exploration, mountain top views, sunrises and sunsets, and much, much more. That's because there is so much beauty, mystery, and wonder in this world. The design of the creation points to a great Designer, and the psalmist says He owns it all. If you grew up looking after cattle, you especially appreciate that the Lord owns the cattle on a thousand hills. But no matter our experience or background, we all can live thankfully, and appreciate the wonder of what the Lord has made and owns. When we know Him as Creator and Savior, His beauty fills our souls. Don't miss it.

Prayer Starter: Lord, help me give you the sacrifice of praise,

____

____

____

in Jesus' name.
~~~~~~~~~~~~~~~~~~~~~~~~~~

LIVING WATER

It was June bugs on a string and sweet smells of honeysuckle. It was cold watermelon and sweet iced tea. It was homemade, banana ice cream churned with a hand crank. It was westerns on a Zenith black and white television that was more furniture than screen. More than anything else, it was really western outside my window. It was at Todd Road that I spent most of my time learning what it was to cowboy. I watched the cowboys ride from dawn to dusk and I learned to throw a leg over from as far back as I can remember. I was always watching and learning.

My Dad and Grandaddy build the first edition of the large, working barn on that old home place. Later, they would add onto it many times, and to me it seemed like some endless cow cathedral of creosoted lumber. The barn was always expanding. Posts were always being added. Something was always going on. They said when I was three I fell down into an eight foot deep post hole, and they could hear me hollering for help but couldn't find me. They finally fished me out, but I don't remember how.

I ran in and out of that old barn, under the belly of good horses, and under and over many a cattle gate. I was always into something. Big hay racks were built for every lot, along with cinder block and concrete water troughs, rigged up with floats to keep 'em full so the cattle could drink. I watched very carefully when they built a larger-than-usual water trough, one that would accommodate two lots through an adjoining, stout, five-board fence. When it was finished, they turned on the faucet and the water poured in. I let it splash over my hands.

It was hot summertime. The grasshoppers were in the fields. The flies were buzzing. The cowboys were singing and the cattle were calling. I wanted to be outside every waking minute, but every afternoon Mama made me take a nap, something I hated to do. I was five years old.

One day, I waited till she made me lay down on the bed and turned on the large box fan in my bedroom. We had no air conditioner back then. It was open windows and fans. The curtains rustled as Mama switched the fan on. When she got busy in the kitchen, I made my move. I pushed up my bedroom window as far as I could. I unhooked the screen and pushed it open, then slid out the window onto the ground. I was free! I was going swimming.

It was one of those still, humid Alabama days when the heat waves rose off the pastures and you could almost drink the air. I walked quickly up the wide gravel lane to the barn. I crawled through the slat fence that surrounding the lot where the new water trough sat. I looked down into the cool, clear water. It was inviting me in.

I pulled off my cowboy boots and hat, my shirt and jeans, then my socks and whitey tighties. I sank down into the three-foot deep trough and it was just as refreshing as I expected. In fact I was in hog heaven. I splashed around in there for about thirty minutes when an old bull walked up to get a drink. I splashed him good and he moved on. Suddenly I heard Mama calling me from the backyard of the house.

I climbed out of the trough, dripping wet and completely naked. I scrambled around and pulled on nothing but my cowboy boots while Mama frantically called out my name in a panicky voice. I ran as fast as I could from the barn to the house. I must have been quite a sight, running buck naked in my cowboy boots, but she was too relieved to scold me...

Fast forward sixty-five years. It's hot summertime and I'm working on a little barn I'm building for our horses here on our place in the country outside Weatherford, Texas. I've sweated through my shirt, jeans, belt and boots. It's a hundred degrees in the shade. That's no exaggeration. You can't drink the air here, it would just scorch your insides.

The sweat drenched my cowboy hat and dripped off the brim and into my face. I move slower in the heat, especially now a days. The horses move slower too. I ran my hand along the withers of my old zebra dun gelding as he walked past me toward the watering trough. I followed him. I looked down into the clear, cool water and it reminded me of a time long ago. I flashed back to Dad's big trough.

I removed my hat and stuck my head into the water. The water ran down the back of my neck, down my face and into my beard. It felt so good, Yep, the water did what it always does- made me feel better. Do you know that feeling? The same happens when you're really thirsty and you get a long, cold drink of it (not out of the horse trough, of course).

Nothing man-made comes close to the quenching relief of clean, clear water. Water is a big deal in the Bible. Jesus was baptized in it, walked on it, and offered to give it to people if they really needed it.

Jesus tells us, in John 4:10, *"If you knew the gift of God and who it is that asks you for a drink, you would have asked him and he would have given you living water."*

Psalm 63:1 says, *"You, God, are my God, earnestly I seek you; I thirst for you, my whole being longs for you, in a dry and parched land where there is no water."*

Matthew 10:42 (NLT) reminds us to give the water to those who thirst. *"And if you give even a cup of cold water to one of the least of my followers, you will surely be rewarded."*

~~~~~~~~~~~~~~~~~~~~~~~~~~

I've been through troubled waters and the Lord rescued me and exchanged my stormy waters for His living water. As in 2 Samuel, 22:17 (NLT), "He reached down from heaven and rescued me; he drew me out of deep waters." I've been through the storms and I understand what it's like to thirst for healing waters. If you are thirsting for something, I pray you learn to thirst for the Lord. If you are parched, only He can quench your soul. If you aren't sure how to find Him, just call on Him and ask. He will answer and give you relief.

My contact information is in the back of this book. If you have questions about the healing grace of our Lord, Jesus Christ, reach out to me. It is my heart's desire to pass the cup to others so their souls may too be quenched.

If you've been saved by His healing waters, remember to pass the cup, my friend.

~~~~~~~~~~~~~~~~~~~~~~~~~

"Jesus answered, "Very truly I tell you, no one can enter the kingdom of God unless they are born of water and the Spirit."
John 3:5 (NIV)

,

"HYDRATE"

The horses, they need water,
The cattle need it, too,
And when things get real hot and dry,
You must use care, it's true.

Overheated, thirsty livestock,
Can really go down quick,
Important they get water,
Or else they could get sick.

Sometimes the heat of summertime,
Makes you feel out of touch,
The soaring temps and dripping sweat,
Can really be too much.

And if you don't just take a break,
Hydrating as you go,
It can really be a problem,
And can happen 'fore you know.

I find in this a lesson,
'Bout what Jesus wants to give,
He called it living water,
And all who drink it live,

Hydrated with the Spirit,
And even when we die,
The river takes us past it,
To our home beyond the sky.

Some don't know what's the matter,
With their weakness and their will,
They're drinking what the world gives,
And never get their fill.

They need the living water,
And here's the best of news,
All who say they're thirsty,
Can get some and they lose,

That desperate, sick old feeling,
Dehydration takes it toll,
But with the living water,
Their lives are on a roll.

So if you're working in the heat,
Be careful, stop and drink,
And if your thirst is spiritual,
Don't wait until you sink,

But come on to the water,
There's plenty, don't you see,
Quenches like no other,
It was always meant to be.

~~~~~~~~~~~~~~~~~~~~~~~~~~~

Jesus said: *"Anyone who drinks this water will soon become thirsty again. But those who drink the water I give will never be thirsty again. It becomes a fresh, bubbling spring within them, giving them eternal life."*
John 4:13-14 (NLT)

When Jesus encountered the Samaritan woman, it was a very unlikely conversation. Racial, religious and gender differences were significant obstacles. Jesus used the occasion to get to the heart of what the woman needed. She didn't need a new man in her life, she'd had plenty. She didn't need clarity on the best place to worship God. She argued with Jesus about that. But she needed living water and that is exactly what He gave her. The entire village was impacted, but more importantly, the one woman with personal problems, relational issues, and spiritual confusion finally got it right. If she can, we can, too. Are you thirsty?

Prayer Starter: Lord, give me the living water of Your Spirit,

____

____

____

____

in Jesus' name.
~~~~~~~~~~~~~~~~~~~~~~~~~~~

ARTISTS

We would like to thank the artists and photographers who gave us permission to include their work in
"Pass the Reins." We often use their art on the God's Horseback Gospel Facebook page as well. God
bless you, one and all.

Steve Boaldin, p. 88

Mary Ross Buchholz, p. 76, 79, 169

Mike Capron p. 50

Dino Cornay, p. 221, 242

Bruce Greene (forward, "What the Cowboys Say")

J.L. Grief, p. 259

Kirstie Lambert, p. 158

Bart Massey, p. 238

Andy Mast, p. 108, 186

Doug Monson, p. 15, 165

Stephanie Roundy, p. 10

Robert "Shoofly" Shufelt, p. 23, 126, 174

Steve Wrubel, p. 59

Gayle Young, p. 247

MEMORIALS

The following are people who had a strong influence in my life and have now crossed over to heaven. They make heaven more real to me than ever.

Paul McClain – my Dad, who raised me in the cattle business, died in 2001.

Deanie McClain Thompson – my Mother, who was the first to tell me about Jesus, died in 2020, age 94.

Laura McClain – my sister, who drowned in a boating accident, 2016.

Roy McClain – my uncle, gospel preacher and mentor, died in 1985.

Mark Eagerton – my good cowboy friend, who died in 2022.

Dr. Millard Box – gospel preacher, a spiritual mentor who died at age 102 in 2019.

Mike Reed – a spiritual mentor who fathered and encouraged me, died in 2022.

Shan McClain – the mother of my children, Tristan, Maggie, Sara Grace and Skyler, died in 2021.

And to all the cowboys who've crossed over to heaven's range and passed the reins to us.

Paul Bradley McClain, Jr. was born in 1952 in Montgomery, Alabama. He grew up in the cattle business, horseback doing cowboy work on his father's ranch. He has taken care of pasture cattle, roped, and worked with young horses. Brad graduated from Texas Wesleyan University in Fort Worth (B.A.) and for a time had a business selling livestock supplements in the Waco area. It was in Texas that Brad felt a strong calling into the ministry and into seminary. Brad graduated from Emory University with a M.Div. and became an ordained pastor. He has traveled across the United States to spread the good news of Jesus and he continues building relationships in every walk of life, especially the cowboy world.

Brad and Stacey live in Texas and Brad is currently involved in various ministries, including Save the Cowboy's Long X Ranch beef ministry, which helps feed hungry families. He has served as an AFCC teacher and pastor. For over 30 years, Brad has served as a church-planter, conference evangelist, consultant, & retreat leader. More than anything, Brad is a follower of Jesus Christ and a true authentic cowboy.

CONTACT INFORMATION

Brad McClain:

Text or call: 251.345.3939

Email: Paulbradleymcclainjr@gmail.com

Donations and/or correspondence can be mailed to:

Brad McClain Ministries

200 S. Oakridge Drive

Suite 101, Box 704

Hudson Oaks, TX 76087

God's Horseback Gospel is a non-denominational outreach of Brad McClain Ministries (501C3), a non-profit ministry approved for tax-exempt donations.